HANDS OFF
MY DAUGHTER
(Until After Marriage)

Protecting our Families in a
Permissive Society

Written and Illustrated
By

BILL PITTENGER

*To Chuck & Sherry Nance,
w/ Love, gratitude + appreciation!*

Bill Pittenger

xulon PRESS

ACKNOWLEDGEMENTS

Many thanks to the following for nit-pick'n editing of my coffee stained manuscript, and for their excellent suggestions, encouragement and patience even as mine was becoming threadbare: Mrs. Dorothy Bain, Mrs. Renate Sprague, Mrs. Sherrie Nance, my wife Shirley, our son, Rick, other credible men (some were incredible), and our daughter, Sandi. I am also grateful to other family members for giving suggestions and granting permission to include *some* of their experiences in this book. I'm thankful to our Lord that in the midst of discouragements and set-backs, He brought positive people to motivate me to keep writing—"Hey Bill! When's that book gonna be printed, anyway? My kids need it!"

PURPOSE

It is my hope that this book will help Christian men accept God's design for the most important government in the world—the home. This is a call for fathers, and potential fathers, to accept responsibility and reject tyranny and passivity; to turn from the ungodly trends of our culture and return to the Bible. When that happens, the Church of Jesus Christ will be more effective in fulfilling our Lord's Great Commission—making disciples of all people (Matthew 28:18-20).

1 Corinthians 11:3 says, *"I would have you know, that the head of every man is Christ; and the head of the woman is the man; and the head of Christ is God."*

PART I

It was clear from Scripture that I am responsible for the oversight and training of our children, but not apart from unity with my wife Shirley. Her counsel and support were indispensable to my position as overseer.

Like all human beings, I have sinned more than I like to admit (Romans 3:23). Like all sinners, I have suffered for my violations (Galatians 6:8). I know that salvation is strictly by grace through faith in Christ's death, burial, resurrection, and ascension (Ephesians 2:8-10). Therefore, if you find some of the things in this book to be painful, know that they were painful for me too (Romans 7:24-8:2). Let's be encouraged that Christ gave us His righteousness—the perfect righteousness of God. With those thoughts in mind, I offer you this book that calls men of all ages to take their divine responsibility seriously.

Brethren, I count not myself to have apprehended: but this one thing I do, forgetting those things which are behind, and reaching forth unto those things which are before, I press toward the mark for the prize of the high calling of God in Christ Jesus (Philippians 3:13-14).

Note: With the exception of family members, all names have been changed. Our children and their spouses gave permission to use their narratives. The personal stories have been reconstructed to the best of my recollection.

OUTLINE FOR PART I

Chapter 1
GOING STEADY
>First Date
>Steady Dating
>Discipline and Probation
>Prayer and Fasting
>Reconciliation

Chapter 2
CIRCLING THE WAGONS
>Personal Dating Standards
>Boys are Different

Chapter 3
COLLEGE LEVEL COURTSHIP
>Dear Mr. and Mrs. Pitt...
>Granting Permission
>Permission Granted
>A Connecticut Yankee Comes Court'n
>Missionaries' Kid (MK)

Chapter 4
COURTSHIP IN A DECAYING CULTURE
>To San Carlos via River Boat
>Practical Bible Studies
>Rick Meets Kara

Chapter 1

GOING STEADY

If any of you lack wisdom, let him ask of God, that giveth to all men liberally, and upbraideth not; and it shall be given him
James 1:6

Our family was vacationing in tropical Santa Cruz, Bolivia for medical attention. Shirley and I were teachers at a missionaries' children school called Tambo, which is located in the semi-arid Andes Mountains about 100 miles west of Santa Cruz. Many missionaries working in this region of South America sent their children to our school to get a structured American education. The mission also had a facility in Santa Cruz we called the mission home. It was here that missionaries and their guests could stay when in the city.

Our older girls Becky and Marilyn, were about to begin their first year of high school. Our son Rick was twelve, and Sandi was seven.

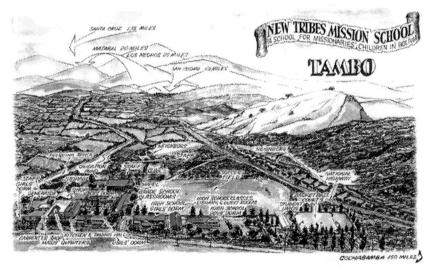

Being a dad and mother had become a greater challenge as our children entered their teens, one after another. Therefore, we began to exercise more freely the privilege of asking God for the wisdom promised in James 1:5. My wife Shirley and I understood the ramifications of our children entering the age when they were capable of reproduction.

The thought that some young man might inappropriately place his hands on one of our daughters before her wedding night began to bother us. We didn't want them caressed and kissed by a variety of men in the absence of any commitment to marriage, nor did we like the idea of our son involved in such activity, either. Nevertheless, we felt social pressure from our culture, and even our peers, to lighten up because romance, as one artist sang, "is a many splendored thing."

This became a critical matter when our oldest daughter entered high school. Her fresh young face and exuberant personality had attracted the attention of a high school senior.

First Date

One afternoon our six-member family was preparing to exit the mission home to do some shopping. I had just bolted the spiked steel-rod gate of the fence surrounding the property. Our oldest daughter chose that moment to tell us that Paul, one of the high school seniors, had asked her for a date. We stopped and listened to our lovely Becky explain why the number one soccer player in our school would take notice of our fifteen year old daughter.

"I really don't care much about him," she said without conviction. "What should I do, Mom? Dad?"

It was small comfort that she didn't "care much about Paul." We knew she was flattered by his attention. Paul was a natural leader in the school, but his leadership was not focused in a positive direction. I was developing a nervous stomach. I stopped, glanced at her mother, then said, "Could you give us some time to think about it?"

Shirley and I were not prepared for romance in our home— except our own, of course. This announcement had come as a surprise to us, which indicated that our heads must have been in the sand. We had not discussed what we would do if one of our daughters wanted to begin dating. The anguish some parents experienced whose teenagers had dated at our school was something we wanted to avoid. The thought of participating in a homemade soap opera made my throat dry.

Nevertheless, that evening Shirley and I decided there would be no harm in Becky having just one date with Paul. He could take her to the restaurant half a block from the mission home. We would chaperone them. We hoped that would be enough to discourage a second date.

So Shirley and I went on a "double date" with Becky and Paul to the *Floresca*, a classy restaurant in a residential neighborhood. They sat at one table, and we sat at another some distance away. I was positioned to observe every move the young man made, but with Shirley's encouragement and prompting I didn't do so.

There was soft Latino music, white tablecloths and napkins, polished silverware, waiters in black coats, pants, bow ties, and crisp white shirts. The servants glided gracefully from table to table with white towels folded neatly over their left forearms as they obsequiously served the diners. A single  red rose graced each table. I had to admit it was an ideal place for a first date.

In fact, it was apparently too ideal. Paul asked if he could have a second double date. Since the first experience went off without a hitch, we decided we could suffer through another steak dinner at the *Floresca*. On each occasion we walked together to the restaurant, and we returned in the same manner. It all seemed quite benign.

Steady Dating

Benign, that was, until we discovered how the experience triggered romantic visions in our daughter's biologically developing mind and soul. When school began, our Becky came to us with another request. Again she quickly sought to put our reservations on ice by saying that she was not really all that excited about Paul. "...but Daddy, Paul wants to begin dating me. You know, go steady. What do you think?"

What did I think? I thought, "This high school senior is going to destroy my mental stability, rob me of sleep, jeopardize my career, destroy our family, and start a revolution in Tambo!" After my face returned to an acceptable ruddy tone, I said calmly, "Honey, we need some time to think about this. Your mother and I want to talk it over."

Shirley and I decided we would give permission provided Becky and Paul agreed to spend less time together than the maximum allowed by the school. The school already had a "no physical contact" policy, as well as other guidelines, but we witnessed the anguish of the parents whose dating children had violated the school's policy.

Our daughter was elated. So was Paul. They began dating, following our instructions. Everything was wonderful. We were beginning to relax a bit.

Discipline and Probation

Within a couple of weeks however, they were seeing each other more each day than our agreement permitted. Shirley and I decided the consequences would be two weeks of prohibition. It was a painful two weeks for them.

Paul appealed to me. "Mr. Pitt, the reason we stepped over the line was because you and your wife are so strict. If we could have the same time together that other couples have, we wouldn't goof up. Please. Can't we have the same time together as the other couples? I promise that you can trust us!"

I reminded him, "Paul, the Bible tells me that he who is faithful in little things will be rewarded with greater things. Keep what you agreed to do, maybe then we can give you and Becky more liberty." (It wasn't exactly a quote from the Bible, but I had the principle right, it seemed).

Prayer and Fasting

The situation did not improve. One day I saw our daughter walking with a group of students, including Paul. With every step she took, our daughter's saucy "body language" was sending a clear message to me, her dad. I thought to myself, "Oh brother, I think I'm in for some rough sledding." (At this point, I would have been a good candidate for a comprehensive course in Proverbs).

I asked advice from my colleagues with whom I shared administrative responsibilities, after explaining what had been going on. They reviewed with me Paul's history of problems that included contempt for his parents and for authority in general.

Ron, Paul's dorm supervisor, was the first to respond. "Bill, I've been making some progress with Paul. Yes, he's had a lot of problems, but I think Becky is good for him. Let's give them some time. Nothing serious can happen over a day or two." (I wasn't so sure).

Ray rather bluntly took a different view. "Bill, you know Paul hasn't changed. He's bad news for your daughter. I say, break them up now!" My friends' conflicting counsel only added to my concern. I tended to favor Ray's opinion.

This was too important a matter to treat as a casual incident, as far as I was concerned. I decided that prayer and fasting was in order since I didn't feel like eating lunch anyway. I strolled along the riverbank and appealed to the Lord for direction.

That afternoon, as we were walking off the soccer field together following P.E. class I asked Becky, "Honey, what's going on with you and Paul?"

"I guess I'm making a decision between you and Paul, Daddy." Her cold matter-of-fact response alarmed me. She was not portraying the respectful daughter I had known Becky to be.

I told Ron and Ray what Becky had said. They immediately agreed with me that Becky and Paul's relationship had to be terminated as soon as possible.

"Thanks fellas! That's all I need to hear." I told Becky and Paul that Shirley and I wanted to talk with them that evening after supper.

It was one thing to be an overseer of someone else's teenaged daughter, like a dorm supervisor, because the final word rests with the parents and the school administration. It's quite another thing dealing with our own daughter, and realizing the final decision rests on my shoulders.

Reconciliation

We were sitting across the dinner table from Becky and Paul when I began the "inquisition." (Time has erased from memory the exact details of our conversation; therefore the following dialogue is only the gist of what was said.)

"Becky," I began, "What have I done to offend you? Is there something that I did that has upset you?"

She thought a moment and then explained that she felt that I had been overly harsh in the way I spoke to her in the classroom that day. She said it was not a serious matter, but it was something that had bothered her.

"Is there anything else?"

"No. I can't think of anything else."

"Will you forgive me for speaking to you that way?"

"Sure Daddy. I forgive you."

I turned to Paul. "Paul, have I done something that caused you to be upset with me?"

Paul thought a moment, and then quietly said, "Yes sir. I feel you've been suspicious of me. I think it has affected your judgment of us."

"Paul, will you forgive me for being overly suspicious of you?"

"Sure, Mr. Pitt."

"Did your mother do anything to offend you, Becky?"

"Oh, no. We're O.K." (Why is it that mothers don't offend as often as dads?)

"How about you, Paul, are you O.K. with Mrs. Pitt?"

"Yes sir. I've no problem with Mrs. Pitt. She's cool."

"That's good. Then we're clear, right?"

They both nodded.

"Well, as you might guess, you've both offended us too. We are not pleased with your attitude toward us regarding the dating matter. Do you think you've been out of line toward us in that?"

Becky responded immediately. "Dad and Mom, will you forgive me for rebelling against you?"

We both responded together, "Sure honey."

Paul followed immediately, "Please forgive me Mr. Pitt! Mrs. Pitt! I'm really sorry I caused you so much trouble."

"Sure, Paul, we forgive you," we replied almost in unison.

Immediately the tension was gone from the room. It was obvious that we had our vivacious Becky back in the fold. After a prayer of confession and thanksgiving, I told Paul and Becky they would have to break up their relationship. Becky seemed to be relieved that it was over.

We learned sometime later that Paul told someone that no adult had ever asked his forgiveness before. That unique experience in our home that evening was apparently a turning point in his life.

Paul became a true friend to Shirley and me. In fact, there was such a change in his life we might have seriously considered him as a potential candidate for courtship of one of our daughters.

That singular experience taught Shirley and me that we needed more of God's wisdom. We went back to the Scriptures to search diligently for principles to guide us, and our teenaged children. We also reviewed materials that helped us locate those principles in the Bible. What we discovered is what we wish to share in this book.

Chapter 2

CIRCLING THE WAGONS

For the weapons of our warfare are not carnal,
but mighty through God to the pulling down of strong holds
II Corinthians 10:4

When pioneers traversing the American western plains would realize they were about to be attacked by hostile Indians, they would circle their wagons for maximum defense.

We realized that, as a family, we needed to "circle our wagons" against the invasion of American culture that seemed poised to take our daughters and son hostage. The immediate need was a defense for our two oldest daughters who were, in my biased opinion, very attractive, and still are. We estimated we had a year or two to plan a strategy for our younger children Rick and Sandi.

A seminar we attended in 1975 focused our attention on biblical principles regarding dating and courtship. The instructor led us to consider several Scripture passages. We were impressed with the instructions found in I Thessalonians 4:3-8, a passage telling Christians how to find a marriage partner God's way.

"For this is the will of God, even your sanctification, that ye should abstain from fornication: 4 That every one of you should know how to possess his vessel in sanctification and honour; 5 Not in the lust of concupiscence, even as the Gentiles which know not God: 6 That no man go beyond and defraud his brother in any matter: because that the Lord is the avenger of all such, as we also have forewarned you and testified. 7 For God hath not called us unto uncleanness, but unto holiness. 8 He therefore that despiseth, despiseth not man, but God, who hath also given unto us his holy Spirit."

Following Becky's dating experience mentioned in chapter one, Shirley and I knew we had to tackle this matter according to God's Word even if it went against our culture. After a careful review of I Thessalonians 4:3-8 Shirley and I asked Becky and Marilyn to have a chat with us about dating. We did not tell the girls that we were opposed to dating. We hadn't come that far in our enlightenment. What we did do was go over these verses in I Thessalonians one verse at a time. Then we asked the girls if they agreed with our interpretation of this passage. They did.

Personal Dating Standards

When we had finished our discussion, the girls wanted to know what they should do when high school boys asked them to go steady. Shirley and I suggested that the girls write out their personal convictions about dating. That way, should a fellow ask one of them to go steady, the potential candidate would know where the lines were drawn. They thought it was a good idea and went to work on it. We helped the girls find additional Scripture verses on the subject.

Not long after that, another fellow sought a dating relationship with Becky. She gave him a copy of her personal dating standards, and waited for his response. The young fellow decided that Becky's standards were not exactly in keeping with his aspirations. As far as we know, that was the only other high school boy who expressed a desire to go steady with one of our daughters. I suppose the word got around because it was a small school.

The girls continued to have individual dates from time-to-time for special occasions like banquets, parties, and dinners. They also had a variety of casual friendships with boys.

Boys are Different

By the time Rick was in high school, he was finding some of the girls attractive. One lovely lady in particular seemed to go for him, and the feelings were mutual. As far as we know, their friendship never quite reached the level of romantic love.

Rick's social experiences with the opposite sex produced some interesting material for discussions with his parents, but we did not sense the same level of disquiet as we did with our daughters. He seemed to be more interested in sports, mechanics, guns, and enjoying the outdoors with his peers and Bolivian buddies. Dating relationships were not on the front burner of Rick's adolescent mind, and, to him, marriage was something people did who had finished college.

After graduating from Tambo's high school our friends in Nebraska offered Rick a job as a farm hand. This included a place to live. They provided a practical education for Rick—farming, operating machinery, truck driving, welding and mechanics.

Surprisingly enough, it was in this small farm community where Rick faced powerful temptations. Rick encountered a culture where booz'n, cruiz'n, and sex were common forms of entertainment for young people, including many who claimed to be Christians. Rick escaped the immoral experiences that would have damaged his future, and we later asked Rick why he didn't accept the opportunities that were offered him by the girls in that town. His response sobered me.

In his deliberate manner, he drawled, "Well, I knew you'd ask me if I was still a virgin. And the thought of that just sobered me up. So, thanks Dad." Rick had some godly men in the church he was attending helping him avoid ruinous decisions. One of those was his pastor who encouraged Rick to enroll in Moody Bible Institute.

All four of our children went through their high school years without the murky complications that steady dating brings into the lives of many teenagers. Like all normal young people, they were attracted to the opposite sex. They even experienced "falling in love," and most all other emotions that are common to teenagers, but they avoided the heart-breaking consequences that result from immoral conduct.

This part of our story could easily have been quite different, as it has been for some of our colleagues and friends who, like us, prayed and sought God's wisdom regarding their children. Our children, like all sons of Adam, are capable of dramatically changing the directions of their lives. No wonder the Apostle Paul wrote, *"Wherefore let him that thinketh he standeth take heed lest he fall"* l (1 Corinthians 10:12).

Life doesn't get easier for our children as they mature. We thought, "They may have made it through their teens without serious emotional, moral, and spiritual wounds, but how will they fare as they become serious candidates for courtship and marriage?"

Chapter 3

COLLEGE LEVEL COURTSHIP

There be three things which are too wonderful for me, yea,
four which I know not:
The way of an eagle in the air;
the way of a serpent upon a rock;
the way of a ship in the midst of the sea;
and the way of man with a maid.
Proverbs 30:18-19

Becky and Marilyn had started first grade together, so they graduated from high school at the same time. Their graduation posed another interesting challenge for these young ladies and their maturing parents. It would not be long before our daughters would experience *"the way of a man with a maid,"* and we tried to *"be anxious for nothing"* in this matter.

Fortunately, it was missionary furlough time for Shirley and me. We were able to be in the United States to help our girls integrate into American society and get jobs. It was a fearful time for them because their work experience had been limited to home and boarding school chores—house cleaning, gardening, laundry, painting, dishwashing, cooking, and the like. However, they soon found employment and learned what it was like to earn wages.

When the time came for Becky and Marilyn to leave the nest for Bible College, they had serious questions for us. "Dad, Mom, what should we do if some guy shows interest in one of us and wants to start dating? What should we say?"

Good questions. They don't call those institutions "bridal colleges" for no reason. Once again, we prayed for wisdom. Since I was the captain of the Pitt Family Ship, I said, "We think you should hold to your standards that you wrote in high school."

"But what if the guy agrees with our standards—how are we going to keep from breaking those standards ourselves?" Another good question.

Somewhere along the line, Shirley and I began to switch from using the word "dating" to the word "courting" or "courtship." We favored a courtship in which a man and woman are seriously considering marriage over dating relationships with a variety of young men; but how can a courtship begin without first having some dates?

I didn't know, but this is what we told our daughters: "Before you agree to begin a serious relationship with a guy, ask him to write for permission from us. If he's seriously interested in you, he'll write. We'll write back asking him to follow the standards we believe God would have you and him follow. We'll explain our reasons—and you'll know what we wrote to him."

"OK, Daddy, but we're scared." They had good reason to be apprehensive. Shirley and I were apprehensive, too.

Dear Mr. and Mrs. Pitt...

We received a letter from a fellow asking for permission to begin a courtship with Becky even before the first semester was out. However, that gentleman didn't "pan out."

By the time we received another letter from a young hopeful, Shirley and I were back in Bolivia. This second fellow also asked for, and received, our permission.

A few months later we received another request. This time the letter was from an MK (missionaries' kid) who had focused his attention on our Marilyn. This son of missionaries also won our approval.

It may seem that the exchanges of letters were smooth and quick, but you must realize that, during this time, we were in a third-world country. Our base was serviced by a mail service that was "snail-mail" in the extreme. One can only imagine how these delays in communication affected our daughters and these men.

Granting Permission

I suppose you are wondering what Shirley and I wrote back to these prospective suitors. Our first letters to each man may have been along the lines of:

"Thank you for your letter in which you expressed an interest in beginning a courtship with our daughter. It speaks well of you that you would even consider writing for permission.

"You probably have noticed that our daughter has some peculiarities and personality flaws. She has most likely discovered you have some interesting imperfections as well.

"We believe that courtship is a time when a young man and woman get to know each other's temperaments and what they are like spiritually. To do that, they must forgo physical affection. That would only confuse their ability to discern what the other person is really like.

"Would you read carefully I Thessalonians 4:3-7? That way you will know what our understanding of these verses is. We believe they are saying the following:

- Verses 3-4 encourages Christian men to obtain wives in a godly and honorable manner
- Verse 5 says that sensual activity—hugging, caressing, and kissing—before marriage is unacceptable before God
- Verse 6 warns that God will punish those who defraud (cheat) by exciting passions that lead to sex outside of marriage
- Verse 7 says that premarital sensuality is unclean and a violation of personal holiness

"We are pleased that you are interested in our daughter as a potential wife, and it is for that reason we want you to get to know each other as well as possible. After marriage it will be too late to reconsider, so God has given us I Thessalonians 4:3-7 as some guidelines. While we realize there are many other Scriptures that touch on this subject, please let us know if you are in agreement with us regarding our understanding of these verses.

"What we have written is not intended to discourage you from getting to know our daughter better. On the contrary, we are hoping that God has led you together, and that you are the person He has for her."

Our objective was not complicated. We simply wanted these young people to get to know each other spiritually. We wanted them to observe each other's relationship with Christ and how dedicated they were to God's purposes. We also wanted them to experience the pros and cons of their temperaments. If they knew each other well before marriage there would be fewer surprises when they became husband and wife. If they did not marry, they would not have violated each other, nor would they have defrauded their future spouses.

Permission Granted

We let out a sigh of relief when we received letters back from the two men. They both agreed with our interpretation of the Scripture passage, and said they would follow the principles in their relationship with our daughters. The missionaries' son had even presented additional verses on the subject. We were impressed!

After the courtship of the two couples had been underway for a time, they began to experience some tension. Our daughters may have been attractive physically, but they also had sinful natures.

We began getting letters from all four of them expressing their frustration over some difficulties they were having. In effect, we responded with Scriptural answers to their requests for advice to resolve their conflicts. We were involved in pre-marital counseling via airmail. In addition, we encouraged them to abide by the rules of the school and seek advice from certain competent and caring staff members that we knew personally.

A Connecticut Yankee Comes Court'n

Shirley and I found it fascinating that Lee Prior, "the young man from Connecticut" who was courting Becky, came on a short-term mission trip to the Ayoré tribe in Bolivia. We learned later that he had two motives in making this trip. One was to serve the Lord, of course, and the other was to meet us. He also planned to ask for Becky's hand in marriage if things went the way he had hoped they would.

Lee was able to make arrangements to travel to Tambo for a visit, and during that time we got to know him quite well. This gave me the opportunity to ask him some important questions. We were impressed with this young man, as were the missionaries with whom he was working at the Ayoré base. Lee took this occasion to ask our permission to marry Becky, and after some time in prayer and discussion, Shirley and I were convinced that God had led Becky to the right guy.

Lee and Becky were able to come to Bolivia so I could perform their wedding ceremony. It was a wonderful event, and their honeymoon was in traveling to various parts of Bolivia.

Since those beginning days, God has given the Priors five beautiful children—four girls and a boy. They have served the Lord in Ivory Coast for twelve years as NTM missionaries, and Lee eventually became a leader on the field. Shirley and I were able to lead a short-term mission team to do a project in the village where they were working. We also became friends with Lee's parents, and his mother has visited their work in Ivory Coast several times.

Missionaries' Kid (MK)

Stephen Bove, the man who was courting our Marilyn had many advantages. Like Marilyn, he had grown up on the mission field, but on the opposite side of the world in Indonesia. Stephen's parents were missionaries to the Punan tribal people of that Southeast Asia country. Stephen had become fluent in the Punan and Indonesian languages, and he knew their cultures well. He had even been "adopted" into the Punan tribe.

In spite of the fact that both Marilyn and Stephen were MKs, they had some rough sledding in their courtship. Stephen discovered that a quiet, insecure girl can have personality quirks and a mind of her own. Stephen also had his share of surprises for Marilyn to sort out.

Nevertheless, as God would have it, Stephen and Marilyn were married in spite of their knowledge of each other's potential for straining a person's emotional stability. We were on furlough on Stephen's and Marilyn's wedding day in Waukesha, Wisconsin at the Faith Bible Church. I remember well the last three words Marilyn said to her mother and me as she gathered her beautiful wedding gown to step up and duck into the car to begin their honeymoon. She turned her head, said goodbye in her rich contralto voice, then added, "Pray for me!" We smiled at this. Her mother understood Marilyn's trepidation better than Stephen or I because Marilyn was about the same age as Shirley was when we got married. *It seems a virgin might ask herself, "What will it be like to be alone all night in the same bed...with a man?"*

There is much more to this story, but we will save some for later. It is enough for now to say that Stephen also sought and received our permission to court and marry Marilyn. I was privileged to participate in officiating Stephen and Marilyn's wedding ceremony, and Stephen's mother was able to leave Indonesia for this wonderful event.

We have noticed over the years that God is vitally interested in what we are doing on earth. He obviously enjoys being involved, and grants wisdom and blessings when asked. *If any of you lack wisdom, let him ask of God, that giveth to all men liberally, and upbraideth not; and it shall be given him* (James 1:5).

Chapter 4

COURTSHIP IN A DECAYING CULTURE

*This know also, that in the last days perilous
times shall come.
For men shall be lovers of their own selves, covetous, boasters,
proud, blasphemers, disobedient to parents, unthankful, unholy.
Without natural affection, trucebreakers, false accusers,
incontinent, fierce, despisers of those that are good.
Traitors, heady, highminded, lovers of pleasures more than
lovers of God;
Having a form of godliness, but denying the power thereof:
from such turn away. For of this sort are they which creep into
houses, and lead captive silly women laden with sins, led away
with divers lusts,
Ever learning, and never able to come to
the knowledge of the truth.*
II Timothy 3:1-7

In the summer of 1993, three young people from our home church joined Destination SUMMIT, New Tribes Mission's short-term mission affiliate. Shirley and I were their team leaders. There were twenty-three high school and college students on our team, and our destination was Paraguay, South America. The students came from a variety of states and Canadian provinces. Our assignment was the renovation of a weather beaten structure for John and Barb Windler, new missionaries to the Angaité (On-guy-TAY) tribe. Barb is Shirley's niece. Windlers' house was a stone's throw from the powerful Paraguay River that meanders through eastern Brazil, southwestern Bolivia, and leaves Paraguay before joining the great Paraná River of Argentina. The humid jungle was either uncomfortably warm and damp, or miserably cold and damp.

Our trip from America to this isolated mission base was memorable even for seasoned travelers like Shirley and me. It began with an all-night delay at Miami airport to await a jet engine generator that never arrived. After several hours in the airplane and the rest of the night in the terminal, we were finally ushered into another plane at sunrise. We missed our connecting flight at Sao Paulo, but a Spanish airline graciously took us on to Paraguay's Guaraní International Airport. (Guaraní and Spanish are the official languages of Paraguay). New Tribes Mission's experienced personnel, who are fluent in both Guaraní and Spanish, guided us through the maze of passport stamping, tipping of officials, baggage handling, and securing for us the privilege to be legal guests of the *República del Paraguay*. Our group was loaded into a variety of vehicles and transported to the mission compound where we bathed and finally collapsed into the beds graciously prepared for our weary bodies. Worse was yet to come.

The following day dawned miserably wet, cold, and depressing. Clouds were at treetop level. We boarded a remarkably modern bus to begin a day and night of swaying and bouncing over uncertain roads to Concepción which is located on the Paraguay River in the center of the nation. Most of us endured the experience in a semi-comatose state. We were in Concepción early the next morning and experienced our first Paraguayan breakfast at a hotel dining room. Shirley and I noticed that several of the girls, including Kara Wilson, were not very hungry. Kara's large, sad eyes and general appearance seemed to be reflecting acute culture shock.

To San Carlos via River Boat

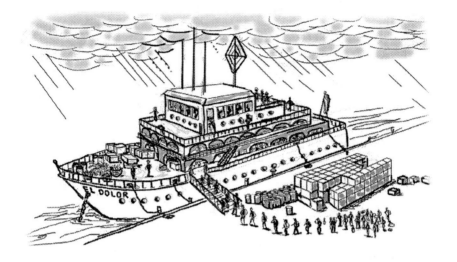

Our team had to continue our travels to the large tribal reserve called *Misión San Carlos*, the Angaité mission base where Shirley's dad, Bob Goddard, Sr., had relocated these people over ten years earlier. The Angaité had for years served as *peones* on large ranches in the Paraguayan Chaco—the notorious "Green Hell" of South America. At San Carlos, each Indian family had access to the river. They were given land of their own on which they could raise crops, fruit trees, and have domestic animals.

New Tribes Mission has airplane service when the weather is favorable, but that day the clouds were heavy with icy drizzle. Alternative transportation was available which meant we would continue to the Angaité tribe via commercial riverboat. At the river pier we somberly viewed the "barque" on which we would place our chilled bodies. It was already heavily loaded with cargo, animals, chickens, and human beings—tribal, Paraguayan, and Brazilian. Since the clouds were hovering just twenty yards above our heads we had no alternative but to walk the plank and join the party. The passengers grudgingly made space for us and our baggage. The students were discovering how they, like prisoners of war, could endure adversity. Kara leaned her head against Shirley's

shoulder and closed her eyes. The ancient craft began lethargically churning upriver aided by the bone-chilling south wind called a *surazo*. The mist found ways to pass by the flapping tarps and increase our misery. Combined odors of urine and cooking wafted up from the bottom deck where the latrine and galley were conveniently located next to each other. The toughest of our group lost all interest in food. I occupied my time sharing the Gospel with Paraguayan men who seemed eager to talk.

Eventually, the boat came to a halt in the river. It was well after midnight and still misting. A smaller open boat operated by New Tribes missionaries came out of the dark and pulled alongside. They had come to ferry us to shore. Experienced hands guided each person safely over a precarious plank secured between the two boats. In spite of our stiff muscles, damp clothes, and the dim lighting, the transition was smooth and rapid.

Within minutes we were all climbing up the steep dark riverbank and led to small buildings that had been prepared for our arrival. We had to wait for sunlight to examine the site where we would spend the next five weeks of our lives. Shirley and I had the luxury of a bed in a two-room cabin, but our team members had the cement floors of two small buildings. With foam mattresses and warm blankets doing what they were designed to do, delicious sleep overcame the weariness of our bodies and souls.

Meanwhile, our son was in Chicago completing his degree at Moody Bible Institute. He had no idea that God was helping him find a "a good thing" and obtain "favor of the LORD." Proverbs 18:22 says, *"Whoso findeth a wife findeth a good thing, and obtaineth favour of the LORD."* God was sending Rick through personalized pre-marital training—managing a multi-racial valet parking crew of a luxury apartment tower to pay for some of his education.

Rick had learned quickly how isolated he had been growing up in rural Bolivia. He discovered there was much more to America than church and attending classes. Much of Rick's "higher education" in the United States took place on a farm in Nebraska. In Chicago he experienced the rich diversity of American culture. Rick shared a bachelors' apartment with an MK from Africa and an Ecuadorian. Perhaps you can understand why Rick majored in international studies.

Practical Bible Studies

Back at the Angaité mission base, I conducted Bible studies each morning and evening. One of the subjects was biblical courtship, a study that seemed to scratch where those young adults itched. I did not realize at the time that I was instructing my future daughter-in-law, but, on the other hand, that possibility had entered my mind since there were several attractive "damsels" on the team.

In the kitchen of our small cabin, Shirley was doing some domestic instruction of her own. We had assigned Kara to work with Shirley. Kara had earlier sat beside me as I was watching a soccer game on the airstrip. She raised her head and rolled her dark saddened eyes up to meet mine and announced, "Bill…, I'm homesick." The healing of the illness was the kitchen assignment. We also made Kara the nurse who passed out homesickness pills to the afflicted—M & Ms, an effective Destination SUMMIT remedy.

With the added help of other girls, all of the meals were prepared in that rustic building. Shirley got to know the girls very well, especially Kara, who was becoming like a daughter to her. They had "hit it off" right from the start.

At one of our nightly meetings, missionary Tony Rogers shared his courtship experience that he had with his wife Rhonda in the 1960s. Tony's dad had noticed Rhonda's vivacious manner and faithful service in their local church. She was attending a Bible college in that community. Tony was also enrolled in another Bible college in another state at the time, but was home with his parents for the weekend.

"Now there's a nice young lady!" Tony's dad exclaimed nodding in Rhonda's direction. "Y' know, Tony, you should get to know Rhonda. She'd made a fine wife for you!" Tony followed his dad's suggestion and dated, courted, and married Rhonda.

Tony's story motivated me to consider that approach with Rick. I had a nice looking candidate in mind for his consideration.

Rick Meets Kara

Rick had moved from Chicago to Chico following his graduation from Moody Bible Institute. He found a well paying job in the logging industry. This employment gave Rick confidence that he could support a wife and family even in Northern California where wages are low and the cost of living is high. Chico, a university and  retirement community is located in an agricultural part of the state where the university, farming, and nursing homes are the main industries.

After Shirley and I returned to Chico, we told Rick about the young brunette college student in our home church who had gone to Paraguay with us. We related that she demonstrated impressive spiritual qualities, that she and her parents were active in our church, and we offered to introduce him to her. We didn't lay it on thick and heavy, but we did suggest that he might enjoy meeting her.

Rick and Kara's friendship began with some sparks. Kara told me what Rick said to her as she got into his car for their first serious date. "What's that you're wearing, fly spray?" She thought he was serious at first but then realized he was afflicted with a sick sense of humor that he used to "tweak" her. He discovered that she too was able to play that game quite well. However, stars in their eyes eventually replaced the sparks.

Within the year a memorable relationship began that honored the Lord and their four parents. Rick and Kara learned much about each other because they followed God's principles in their courtship.

There was a time, however, when Rick and Kara were uncertain about continuing the courtship. They both felt insecure about marriage and just avoided the subject. Rick, as it turned out, was fearful of losing Kara should he ask her to marry him, and Kara was unsure because she was ten years younger than Rick.

(The following excerpt may not be perfectly accurate, but I thought you might enjoy my version of it).

It seems that a friend asked Rick one day why he didn't ask Kara to marry him. "Rick, she's a nice one! What's hold'n ya up, man?" So Rick told him some of his concerns.

Well, this friend was a bit on the direct side so he let loose this word of admonition. "Look, ole buddy, ya gotta pursue marriage like when yer head'n for the mill! She's the one ya want, isn't she?"

"Uh, well yes! She's the *only* one I want."

"Well, tell her, and don't beat around the bush about it. Ya gotta be a man about this and stick yer neck out. Whatcha got to lose? She can only say no."

It was interesting that Rick was receiving a similar message from Shirley and me on assignment in Singapore. We were not quite so direct, however.

So Rick "stuck his neck out," and went before his future father-in-law to ask approval for Kara's hand in marriage. Then Rick popped the "Big Q," and Kara said, "Yes, Rick. I will."

Rick and Kara had a beautiful wedding with a large gathering of family members and friends, including Rick's roommate from

Bible College who was his best man. Our pastor, who performed their ceremony, had been a missionary in Cochabamba, Bolivia, and that seemed special to our family because Rick was born in that city. When the preacher asked for the bride's ring, Rick's best man pulled out a set of handcuffs.

It had cost Rick hundreds of dollars in international calls seeking our counsel and keeping us abreast of developments. He honored us in this way, and he also honored his future wife's parents by getting to know them well. Rick gained their respect by demonstrating appropriate leadership during his and Kara's courtship experiences. He had waited until he had graduated from college, had proven to himself that he was ready to take a wife, and that he was able to lead and support a family. We believe Rick and Kara also honored their heavenly Father by following His principles in their pre-marital relationship.

Chapter 5

THE FLIP SIDE

He [or she] that is unmarried careth for the things that belong to
the Lord, how he [or she] may please the Lord
I Corinthians 7:32b

Our youngest daughter is still single at this writing; therefore we will focus on the challenges affecting Christian single girls and women in our culture.

Around 56 AD the Apostle Paul, under the inspiration of the Holy Spirit, told the Corinthian believers that singleness was better than marriage if the person was able to control his/her passions (See I Corinthians 7:7-9). This Scripture puzzled me until I observed the affects President Lyndon B. Johnson's "Great Society," his "War on Poverty," and the Vietnam War Era had on our nation. This once powerful politician's policies brought upon our nation an acceleration of degradation almost unequaled in our nation's short history.

LBJ

As part of my masters program through Chico State University in 1975, I focused on the counter-culture movement's influence on the local churches in Northern California. Promiscuity, co-habitation, divorce, and abortions were becoming prevalent among Christians and commonplace in the culture as a whole. This moral decline also affected the lives of some of the missionaries' children.

America was reaping the consequences of this cultural upheaval when we and our youngest daughter, Sandi, returned

to the United States from Bolivia in 1987. Since Sandi would be enrolling in a secular high school, Shirley and I felt it was necessary to be more culturally attentive than seemed necessary for our older daughters.

Sandi was as aware as we were about the moral decline in America. She felt free to express her views on these matters because we encouraged discussions on all issues that were pertinent to our family. No subject was off limits.

Sandi Goes to College

After prayer, family discussions, and making comparisons of the options available to her, Sandi decided she wanted to become a grade school teacher and attend a Christian college. Shirley and I were well acquainted with various universities and colleges on the West Coast because of our responsibilities as representatives. Collectively we settled on a conservative, four-year Christian college with a reputation for sound Bible doctrine. The school also provided a degree in education and state certification.

Check'n the Herd

During Sandi's college years, several fine young men showed serious interest in her. Some were tall, some short, some hefty, others thin. There were the curly haired, straight haired, and a few were losing hair while others were already turning gray around the edges. One had large sweaty hands with thick fingers that caused Sandi's hand to go to sleep when they intertwined their fingers on a date. Another fellow was about Sandi's height—five-foot-two, but agile and mild-mannered. They all seemed to be doctrinally acceptable, but varying in degrees of knowledge, maturity, and commitment. Some drove nice cars, and others had nothing but a large school debt. A few had been around the block too many times, and others were still "wet behind the ears." One clean cut fellow, somewhat on the nerdy side, had a shiny yellow VW bug which I admired, but his attributes didn't measure up to what Sandi was hoping for. Her body language and "ahems" reminded me that ultimately she was the one that had to live with Mr. Christian Whoever.

One fellow seemed to fit the bill though. Brad was active in cross-cultural ministry, personable, manly (hair on chest), had a nice sense of humor, enjoyed coffee, was quite handsome, and of average height (she didn't check his dental work). Sandi took some of the same classes with Brad, and they were both involved in a college outreach program. They got to know each other well enough to create a bit of "chemistry." When she introduced him to us we thought Sandi had a winner! We enjoyed our short visit with Brad. Later, however, she was cautioned by godly advisers who knew Brad was not ready to assume the responsibilities of a husband. Sandi accepted this advice and was willing to give Brad some time to deal with a character deficiency, but there was little evidence he was succeeding.

Sandi continued to have a variety of dates but no serious prospects. So she graduated and began her career as an elementary school teacher.

Slimmer Pick'ns

As our culture continues to slip and slide leftward, we've noticed a growing number of older men and women singles in local churches, but how many are eligible to marry virgins? Divorce, fornication, pornography, and substance abuse have affected many Christian singles over eighteen.

Increasingly, more "Christian" young people discard their priceless virginity because "everyone's doing it." This is not new; it's the same old idolatrous "doctrine of Balaam" which, in short, is "join the crowd" (Read Revelation 2:14 and consider Numbers chapters 22-24).

The good news is many singles remain chaste, including widows and widowers in spite of the decline. These are disciples who have presented their bodies *a living sacrifice, holy, acceptable unto God"* (See Romans 12:1-2). Now, if we can just find a way to get them all together. How about a website called "Ye Old Hitching Post.Com."

Family Protection

Sandi assured us that she was thankful she had a family she could trust to give her sound counsel when faced with serious decisions. Through the years, she has sought her dad's protection when her emotions ran high, and looked to her mother for female empathy.

One night as we were talking about this chapter, Sandi said, "Dad, did you know there are girls who envy me?"

"How's that?" I asked.

"I was talking with a single girl who knows you've been there for me even in my adult years. She wishes her dad would respond to her need for his involvement regarding relationships with men."

"Well, she has her mother and friends, doesn't she?"

"Oh, sure, but it's not the same. There's nothing quite as reassuring as when your dad takes an interest in your stories, offers sound advice, and comforts you when you're feeling insecure. I don't know many fathers who understand how important this is to daughters."

The responsibility to provide these things for my daughter motivates me to pursue God's principles in the Scriptures to the best of my ability, and to seek the combined counsel of her mother and brother. Sandi told us that she does not sense a need to seek counsel from any others regarding dating and courtship, even though she realizes there are trustworthy Christians who give sound biblical advice. She has read many books on the subject. In fact, she would make an excellent mentor herself; she is very informed.

Serving Single

We have "been there" for our daughter throughout the years, not to dictate or manipulate, but to pray, discuss, counsel, and mentor whenever she desired our involvement. At this writing,

she still expresses her need for parental guidance in her life even though she is a mature professional adult. She has often expressed how grateful she is to have our fellowship. Sometimes the international phone calls from Quebec, and then Ivory Coast, had been expensive, but well worth the investment. She has returned to California and is presently teaching in a Christian school in Orland, California.

Sandi does not wish to remain single, but she has left that matter in the hands of her Heavenly Father. She is confident that her *"LORD God is a sun and shield: the LORD will give grace and glory: no good thing will he withhold from them that walk uprightly"* (Psalm 84:11).

Singleness of Heart

In regards to being single, it helps to read I Corinthians 7:28: *"If thou marry, thou hast not sinned; and if a virgin marry, she hath not sinned. **Nevertheless such shall have trouble in the flesh: but I spare you.**"* Verse 34 says, *"There is difference also between a wife and a virgin. The unmarried woman careth for the things of the Lord, that she may be holy both in body and in spirit: but she that is married careth for the things of the world, how she may please her husband"* (emphasis added).

Is singleness a difficult thing for Sandi? At times; however, she is a contented and pleasant person who has discovered the joy of living for Christ and investing her energies in the lives of children.

Chapter 6

PREPARING CHILDREN FOR ADULT LEVEL CHALLENGES

Train up a child in the way he should go:
and when he is old, he will not depart from it
Proverbs 22:6

Someone may respond, "It's nice that your kids developed godly standards and followed them, but it sounds sugar-coated to me. Didn't they experience rebellion, disappointments and broken hearts?" Of course they did, but I am not going to "tell all" because it would not be appropriate. I can say, though, our children accepted our Bible based convictions, followed our instructions *imperfectly,* and reserved their priceless virginity until marriage.

Our Heritage

Thanks to the excellent home training and Bible teaching Shirley and I received, our children did not experience the "terrible twos" or the "rebellious teens." We owe a lot to our parents, grandparents, and to a variety of faithful Christian men and women who had a part in shaping our lives. Like you, we had many people influence us for good—schoolteachers, principals, policemen, friends, and neighbors. God had them everywhere.

Doth not wisdom cry? and understanding put forth
her voice? She standeth in the top of high places,
by the way in the places of the paths. She crieth

at the gates, at the entry of the city, at the coming in at the doors. Unto you, O men, I call; and my voice is to the sons of man. O ye simple, understand wisdom: and, ye fools, be ye of an understanding heart (Proverbs 8:1-5).

Pre-puberty Instruction

Often, the children were the ones who initiated the education process by asking questions like, "Mommy, where do babies come from?" Shirley and I sensed where the lines were drawn regarding who should be the instructor on certain delicate subjects.

Before our children reached puberty, Shirley and I had prepared them for the transition into youthful adulthood. We had learned from others that it was important to be first in teaching the kids about the "birds and the bees." We knew we could not prevent them from getting information from their peers, but we could beat the peers to the punch. We also sought to protect them from government school sex-education because this delicate subject is the responsibility of parents.

Post-puberty Instruction

When our children reached puberty we were careful to discuss certain essential issues with them before they entered the world of relationships with the opposite sex. As a starter, here are some of the issues we felt were important for our children to understand at that time:

- How boys and young men are "programmed" by God for assertive reproduction
- How ladies are particularly different from men in their physiological make-up and responses to physical intimacies

- Why natural attraction to the opposite sex is not that which holds a marriage together
- How *agape* (Greek for charitable love) and *philandros* (fondness) strengthens the marriage and increases when *agapao* (acts of kindness) and *phileo* (appreciation) are consistently given
- How *agapao* and *phileo* can be practiced during the courtship without *eros* (sensual excitement)

Teaching Incrementally

We did not go into detail when the kids were in their early teens, but as they got older we reviewed some of the same territory, but more specifically. We taught incrementally—according to the need for additional information. We discovered that the supper table was a good place for such an education. It was fascinating how much detail we could cover without embarrassing one another.

Our children believed us when we told them of the dangers of "dating around." We had established a rapport with them when they were small and explained what happened among those who had one partner after another. Most significantly, we showed them what the Bible had to say on the subject.

Of course, our instruction did not take from them the natural attraction they felt toward potential candidates. Potential candidates had to wait until proper maturity before considering serious dating and courtship. Nevertheless, a few tried pushing the envelope and put a hairy toe into dangerous territory.

Avoiding the "Dating Game"

For the most part, our children did not experience the emotional trauma of entering serious relationships with the opposite sex and "breaking up." They enjoyed casual friendships, with many young people of both sexes during their teens (except for Becky's brief experience).

As you might suspect, Becky, Marilyn, Rick, and Sandi had normal emotional frustrations and disappointments during their years of early adulthood—ages thirteen to seventeen. I'm sure they even "fell in love" at times. From our observations, their frustrations and disappointments were nothing compared to the problems some of their peers were experiencing. They also faced rejection by some of their peers because of these standards, and possibly because the peers knew Dad was involved.

No Generation Gap

As teenagers our children observed the so-called "generation gap" between young adults and their parents that the media promoted during the Vietnam War era and succeeding decades. They did not participate in that rebellion; on the contrary, our children disdained the raucous anti-authority culture. It was not because our kids did not have problems with their attitudes; they were normal descendents of Adam and Eve, just like their parents. However, all four of them were blessed with biblical training that came through their parents who themselves had the benefits of godly parents and wise counselors. Also, missionary colleagues, Bolivian friends, Bible teachers, and so many others have had positive influence in our children's lives. The children could have rejected biblical wisdom, but they did not.

God honored His Word, gave grace to us all as we all *confessed our sins* to our heavenly Father. We were learning to acknowledge our offenses against each other and to as*k for forgiveness*. We did it *often*, sometimes several times in one day.

Chapter 7

SOME COURTSHIP PERKS

There be three things which are too wonderful for me,
yea, four which I know not:
The way of an eagle in the air;
the way of a serpent upon a rock;
the way of a ship in the midst of the sea;
and the way of a man with a maid
Proverbs 30:18-19

Courtship is a time to anticipate leaving Dad and Mom and "cleaving" to your future wife. Any young man "worth his salt" wants to be independent, but God has designed us fellows to hanker for a suitable helper. When she finally shows up on the scene, she has a tendency to make life interesting, you know, something like sweet and sour chicken—delicious but a bit tangy. Therefore, God has programmed us men to find a girl who will have us so that together we can begin a new family. The Apostle Paul reminds us, "*For this cause shall a man leave his father and mother, and shall be joined unto his wife, and they two shall be one flesh* (Ephesians 5:31).

Long Distance Mentoring

An important thing developed after Lee and Stephen began courting Becky and Marilyn—they all continued to correspond with Shirley and me and asked for our counsel. The men seemed to realize that our commitment to God's standards reflected our devotion to Christ and His Word. Lee especially sought our advice during his courtship, and this continued even after he married Becky. Stephen also sought our counsel, but not as frequently because he had a close relationship with his missionary parents who helped him with the challenges he was experiencing with Marilyn.

Both Becky and Marilyn provided frequent updates concerning their relationships with the fellows. These included some descriptions of the men's qualities, the girls' personal moments of insecurity, their doubts, and the special moments that only those in love can fully appreciate. No one writes novels that could better captivate our interest than these wonderful letters.

Stephen's Story

Several years later, Stephen, who is a talented storyteller, enjoyed filling us in on some of the experiences he shared with Marilyn during their courtship. I'll attempt to tell you one of these stories as I remember it.

In his pursuit of greater spiritual maturity, Stephen had been reading about loving our enemies and being kind to unlovable people. Therefore, he looked for someone in the school that he might find difficult to love, someone he could practice loving in the manner addressed in the Bible in spite of his natural inclinations.

Stephen had been observing Marilyn's "body language" as she entered the school dining hall and took her seat. She would walk straight through the open French doors into the crowded hall without glancing to the left or the right. She primly took her place at the table without acknowledging anyone, and throughout the meal she addressed the others with a cursory exchange, such as, "Pass the gravy please." After finishing her meal, she left in the same manner in which she entered. To Stephen, this girl was one of the haughtiest and most aloof girls he had ever seen. He thought she might be the ideal candidate to test his calling to show love to an obviously unlovable person. (Stephen *must* have had mixed emotions, because Marilyn is a very attractive person, in my biased opinion).

They both enrolled in Bible Memory Class, so it was there that Stephen decided to make his attempt at *agapao* love by writing little messages to her. He left a note accompanied with a half-stick of gum. The note simply said "Hi."

Someone's playing a trick on me, Marilyn thought, but her curiosity got the best of her. She glanced around the classroom and made eye contact with Stephen who had a revealing grin on his face.

Another day, another note—"Hi! How are you?"

She wrote back, "Fine, how are you."

Hey, I think we have something going here, Steve thought.

Marilyn was in a quandary. *What shall I do? This guy is showing attention to me. What about the promise I made to my parents when this happens?*

Some days later, Marilyn wrote, "I want to see you after class."

Stephen thought, *oh brother, I'm going to get it now. She's offended, and she's going to tell me to get lost.* Later, at work that day Stephen was plagued with negative thoughts.

That evening, near "The Coke Room" where they had agreed to meet, Stephen sat down beside Marilyn on a bench provided for moments like these.

He glanced at her out of the corner of his eye and stated, "Well, here I am." She didn't look at him.

He wasn't quite prepared for what came from the lips of this perplexing, blonde-haired woman. She looked straight into his eyes and asked, "Are you interested in dating me?"

Stephen's eyes grew large. He hesitated a long time—about ten to twenty seconds. He felt he had been blindsided. He was caught off guard, but finally stammered, "Uhm, uh... Well... Yeah... Uh, yes, I *am* interested." (He told me that until then he had never seriously thought of her as a potential candidate, at least in a romantic way).

Marilyn continued, "Well, then, you will have to write to my dad to ask for permission to begin a relationship with me. I promised my parents not to begin dating someone unless the guy is willing to ask for permission."

Stephen was flabbergasted by this, but he wrote for permission within two or three days.

(When I went over this story with Stephen and Marilyn, I learned that it was embarrassing for Marilyn to ask Stephen to write for permission. She knew of no others at the school that followed this procedure, but Stephen said he was "cool" with the idea.)

Before the story above took place, Shirley and I had come to Waukesha, Wisconsin where the Bible college was located to visit the girls just before returning to Bolivia. Rick and Sandi were with us.

At that time, Becky was dating the first fellow who had asked permission, but Marilyn was not dating anyone. We had a Sunday meeting at a church in Kenosha, Wisconsin where my cousin was pastor. Becky and Marilyn decided to accompany us because we were planning to continue on to Miami the next day, and then on to Bolivia. The fellow that was courting Becky and another fellow had decided to go along. That second fellow was Stephen Bove. Stephen had been dating a girl, so I was wondering why he had come along. I suspected he was interested in Marilyn.

After church that evening, we all went to a restaurant. Shirley talked with Becky and Marilyn, and I decided to talk with Becky's boyfriend and Stephen. Since both men were potential sons-in-law (one never knows), I wanted to cover the dating, courtship, and marriage principles that seemed ever-present in my thinking those days. Both men gave me their full attention. Stephen's little story written above took place within a few months after our visit at the Kenosha restaurant.

Pre-and-Post-Marriage Counseling

That our future sons-in-law would ask for our advice regarding the challenges they were experiencing with our daughters seems to justify courtship. It was a special privilege to give biblical and subjective responses to their questions. Even after marriage, we have had correspondence on a variety of serious issues affecting their lives. These young men honored Shirley and me by including us among their mentors and counselors before and after marriage.

Other Cultures

We took two SUMMIT teams of Singaporean university students to tribal areas—a team to the Philippines and the other to Thailand. One of the subjects we taught our Asian team members was biblical dating, courtship and marriage. Their interest was very high because they were all single and contemplating future careers and marriage. Eventually, several of the team members asked us to be their mentors and counselors when they entered a serious relationship with a potential marriage partner. They continued to seek our counsel after they were married, and that marriage-counseling ministry continues to this day.

Courtship, Marriage, and Ministry

World evangelism is the primary privilege of Christians who are *committed* disciples. Therefore, we searched for faithful people in whom we could invest our lives (II Timothy 2:2). It was our desire to prepare our children and all young people we influenced to present their bodies as living sacrifices to our God and Savior, and to discipline their minds to resist the appeals of our humanistic culture (Romans 12:1-2). To qualify for effective Christian ministries, such as missions, we knew they had to sanctify the Lord God in their hearts (I Peter 3:5). If they understood and followed I Thessalonians 4:1-7 in their pre-marital experiences with the opposite sex, we believed they would also follow our Lord in all other areas of their lives. Godly dating, courtship, and marriage principles have that kind of significance. The following chapters will explain why that is the case.

NOTES

NOTES

PART II

Now you know some of the challenges my wife and I experienced with our children as we endeavored to prepare them for marriage and protect them in the process. In the following chapters I will state our Bible based convictions and the benefits that come from following these convictions. You will see how we struggle with our enemies—*the world, the flesh and the devil*—and how God gives victory over them.

You may be surprised how significantly dating, courtship and marriage are connected to personal holiness and our Lord's Great Commission. As ambassadors for the King of Kings in a fallen world there is much at stake, and the battles sometimes get rough.

For your benefit I have given you an outline of these chapters so you can go directly to these various subjects, or read them sequentially.

OUTLINE FOR PART II

Chapter 8
AVOIDING MORAL DISASTERS
>   Adam's Idol
>   Adam's Sexuality
>   Controlling the Tiger
>   Dads Can Protect Their Daughters
>   Priceless Virginity
>   The Hymen
>   An Honorable Father

Chapter 9
YOUR SON VS THE WORLD
>   Preparation for Spiritual Warfare
>   Forgiveness for Failures
>   Pornography
>   It's all in Your Head
>   Porn in the Pulpit
>   Valuable Virginity
>   A True Disciple
>   Protecting Our Sons

Chapter 10
FINDING GOD'S WILL
>   Sanctified Dating and Courtship
>   "Positional" and "Personal" Sanctification
>   A Strange Sign
>   What about the Hebrew Ladies?
>   God's Plan to Execute Moses
>   Circumcision of the Heart
>   Pop Porn vs. God's Men

Chapter 8

AVIOIDING
MORAL DISASTER

If thou marry, thou hast not sinned;
and if a virgin marry, she hath not sinned
I Corinthians 7:28

Our daughters were naturally drawn to the opposite sex. How were we going to help them keep their virginity for godly men who had saved themselves for our daughters?

This question led naturally to other questions such as, what if the godly man came to Christ *after* he had given his virginity to another girl? Would we want our daughter to marry someone who had such an experience? What does the Bible say about that? What should be our position toward a Christian man who had committed fornication after salvation? Does his repentance qualify him as a candidate to court our virgin daughter?

We did not have our heads in the sand regarding young men. After all, I was a young man myself, and I knew what went through the minds of the majority of them. I know what went through mine! The truth of the matter is Adam's descendants have major problems when it comes to sexuality. That includes Christians too. Of course that goes for the Eves of this world as well, but Eve's challenges are somewhat different than Adam's.

What started out so wonderful for Adam when he first saw Eve is far from what we experience today.

Adam's Idol

The human race's skewed view of sexuality began in the Garden. We are told in Genesis that Satan deceived Eve by telling her she could have the wisdom of God if she ate the "forbidden fruit." She got the knowledge all right, but she got a lot more than she expected.

She also put Adam in a tough spot by forcing him to make a decision. Would he follow Eve and eat the fruit, or would he stay true to God and hope for another to take Eve's place? He chose to go with Eve!

Why did he do it? Apparently, he loved her! After all, she was the most beautiful woman in the world! The fact is Adam chose to love Eve more than he loved God. By doing that, he committed the first sin of idolatry. Eve became his idol,

and he was apparently willing to die for her. God later revealed that idolatry violates the first of the Ten Commandments, which, of course, were not given to people until Moses received them personally from God Himself. Adam was a prototype idolater.

Adam's Sexuality

Adam's sin very directly affected every human being that has descended from him and Eve. The consequences of Adam's sin appear to be especially manifest in the area of men's sexuality.

Adam's idolatry resulted in dynamic changes in his attitude, his behavior, and his affections. These changes were passed on to us, his descendants, producing complications that cause confusion in the hearts of men. We naturally look upon women with a mixture of legitimate desire and hopeful anticipation. Unfortunately, self-centered passion seems to corrupt our envisioned ideal even though we are seeking that beautiful experience Adam had with Eve before The Fall.

Men pursue lust even though they have in their hearts the Law of God that warns them that something is amiss. Honorable men, Christians and non-Christians alike, know the dangers of this propensity and prudently avoid the pitfalls. Many actually enjoy the blessings God has for faithful men who love their wives unselfishly, and become great providers, protectors, and role models for others hoping to find Eves of their own.

Controlling the Tiger

When we fellows were immature youths, we might have imagined in our minds and hearts the beauty of a loving relationship with that special girl we hoped to find one day. However, after we passed through puberty there arose a tiger in us that we can call sexual desire. The tiger was just a cub until we were about twelve or thirteen, but after puberty's transformation, sexual desire came upon us with all of its potential for good and evil. It confused the ideals we had envisioned as children.

After puberty, young adult men become fascinated with women's bodies, especially their breasts. (In some cultures, breasts may take a back seat to other parts of a woman's anatomy. Thighs, I understand, are the focus among some African cultures.) With just a lingering thought on the face and body of the subject, men often sense chemical activity producing embarrassing action in their bodies—embarrassing, that is, if someone else knows what is going on.

Job was a married man who addressed this problem when he said, *"I made a covenant with mine eyes; why then should I think upon a maid?"* (Job 31:1). Job realized that it was through his eyes that temptations would come into his brain regarding a young woman. So, knowing that men are most vulnerable sexually by way of the eyes, Job made a commitment with his eyes that he would not use them to lust after a desirable woman.

Why the eyes, since they are only physical parts of his body? Why not make the covenant with the Lord? Job realized that only his personal determination would keep him from sinning, not a covenant with the Lord. Therefore, he determined to guard his eyes from bringing tempting messages to his *brain*. Job also knew that his *mind* was where the battle raged (Cp. Romans 12:2).

In contrast, King David failed to keep his tiger in check when he *saw* Bathsheba bathing her nude body on the flat roof of her hut.

Samson also allowed his tiger to dominate him, and it cost him his eyeballs and freedom.

The Apostle Paul said, *"I [control] my body, and bring it into subjection: lest that by any means, when I have preached to others, I myself should be a cast away"* (I Corinthians 9:27).

Christian men know their sexual appetite is God given, but Adam's sin has changed God's original design. Therefore, we must be taught to keep that tiger caged or we are in for serious trouble spiritually, and sometimes, legally. In fact, it could even lead to physical death via disease, execution, or murder (Proverbs 7:6-27).

Girls, I've been told, don't experience the same thing we are experiencing, though we might foolishly try to imagine what they are thinking. When we marry, we discover how differently women are wired emotionally and sexually. It is quite a revelation. For a godly man seeking wisdom, however, discovering the differences between himself and his Eve can be a delightful revelation.

Dads Can Protect Their Daughters

What we know about ourselves makes us dads best qualified to protect our daughters from the tigers—or should I say wolves? I do not see all men as wolves whose objective in life is to steal young women's virginity. There are many wise men both young and old. Nevertheless, I do understand that the sons of Adam have a tiger in their tank that could draw any one of them into some form of deviant behavior. Therefore, wise young men will recognize their need for authority over them.

All men need authority that will help them keep their tiger in its cage when it comes to courting our daughters, and Dad is the best qualified for that position. He knows all about the tiger. The Bible has given us the right balance on this subject of protecting our daughters ... *and* their mothers. This conviction, however, comes from understanding the principles God has given us throughout the Bible beginning with Noah and Abraham. Mothers are not *equally qualified* to give that protection. Their limitations may not seem obvious to you, but there are critical limitations. Some individuals may insist that the mother is equally qualified. However, I believe they are deceived because of their ignorance of God's design (Consider Genesis 2:18 and I Timothy 2:13-14). Mom adds power to Dad's authority because God designed her to be Dad's helper. The "wisdom" of our generation, unfortunately, has produced unbearable burdens that the ladies were never designed to carry. Note: I did not say that mothers do not play an important role in this matter. You'll see that is not my position as you read on.

Priceless Virginity

Godly men understand how priceless is the gift of virginity that young couples give to each other on their wedding night.

Humanists may ask, "What's the big deal about a girl's virginity?" Well, God has a lot to say about it! For one example, a girl who gives her body to a man who is not her husband is called a whore in Scripture (Deuteronomy 22:21). I know that is strong language. God spoke through His Hebrew prophets on this subject. God set the standard for moral purity, and violations of His standard always result in severe, life-changing consequences. Aren't you glad He is also the God of mercy and love who can give "beauty for ashes"?

God had Isaiah write:

> *"To comfort all that mourn;*
> *to appoint unto them that mourn in Zion;*
> *to give unto them beauty for ashes,*
> *the oil of joy for mourning,*
> *the garment of praise for the spirit of heaviness.*
> *That they might be called trees of righteousness,*
> *the planting of the LORD,*
> *that he might be glorified"*
> (See Isaiah 61:1-3 emphasis added)

Few things can take the wind out of Dad's sails like the loss of his daughter's virginity before her wedding. A father knows that the man involved was probably self-centered, undisciplined, and hungry for self-gratification. The loss of a daughter's virginity before marriage means she is a used article with seriously diminished value in the eyes of many men. However, God does not have the mind of men, and He sees her as a precious jewel who can be redeemed by the Blood of the Lamb.

In a similar way, a godly father would grieve at the loss of his son's virginity to a foolish girl.

> *"My son, keep my words,*
> *and lay up my commandments with thee.*
> *Keep my commandments, and live;*
> *and my law as the apple of thine eye.*
> *Bind them upon thy fingers,*
> *write them upon the table of thine heart.*
> *Say unto wisdom, Thou art my sister;*
> *and call understanding thy kinswoman:*
> *That they may keep thee from the strange woman,*
> *from the stranger which flattereth with her words"*
> (Proverbs 7:1-5)

The Hymen

God designed a girl in such a way that she could prove her virginity on her wedding night.

First, I need to talk about making vows. In the Old Testament, we observe that a solemn covenant between two people was accompanied by the shedding of a clean animal's blood, e.g., a lamb. God did this with Abraham (Genesis 15:7-17). Making solemn vows was very serious business in the Old Testament as one can see by reading Leviticus 22:20-25.

Now, let's get back to a virgin daughter's wedding night. There is a membrane, called the hymen, in a virgin's birth canal. God put it there to protect her reputation. This membrane is filled with blood vessels and is broken when the virgin has her first sexual intercourse with her husband.

God gave Israel the following law to protect a virgin bride from a false accusation.:

> *"If any man take a wife, and go in unto her, and hate her, and give occasions of speech against her, and bring up an evil name upon her, and say, I took this woman, and when I came to her, I found her not a maid. Then shall the father of the damsel, and her mother, take and bring forth the tokens of the damsel's virginity unto the elders of the city in the gate. And the damsel's father shall say unto the elders, I gave my daughter unto this man to wife, and he hateth her; and, lo, he hath given occasions of speech against her, saying, I found not thy daughter a maid; and yet these are the tokens of my daughter's virginity.*
>
> *"And they shall spread the cloth before the elders of the city. And the elders of that city shall take that man and chastise him. And they shall [fine] him in an hundred shekels of silver, and give*

them unto the father of the damsel, because he hath brought up an evil name upon a virgin of Israel: and she shall be his wife; he may not put her away all his days.

"But if this thing be true, and the tokens of virginity be not found for the damsel, then they shall bring out the damsel to the door of her father's house. And the men of her city shall stone her with stones that she die: because she hath wrought folly in Israel, to play the whore in her father's house: so shalt thou put evil away from among you" *(Deuteronomy 22:13-21).*

The night a man and his bride come together, there is the shedding of blood, the blood of a virgin who has reserved herself for her husband! We might conclude, then, that this shedding of blood was God's way of sanctifying the solemn vows between the young virgin husband and his virgin wife. No wonder a Hebrew girl would preserve her intimacies for only one man!

Interestingly, the word "hymeneal" refers to a wedding or marriage (American Heritage Dictionary). Can we say, then, that a true wedding is called a "hymeneal experience"? Isn't it also a God-designed *sacrifice* of the girl's virginity when her marriage is consummated, thus sanctifying the physical union?

(Note: The hymen may be broken accidentally by physically demanding sports activities, by the use of tampons, or by an initial pap smear. It is not uncommon for women to be born without a hymen.)

Heavy indeed is the realization that one's daughter has lost her virginity before marriage. She sacrificed a precious possession—a gift that she could have given her husband on the night she was wed. She and her husband would never know the joys of two virgins uniting in physical intimacy. Before God, it is equally distressing for a son to give his priceless virginity to someone other than his bride.

What young Christian man would not want to marry a virgin? Even many non-Christians want that! What normal Christian father would not want his daughter and son to marry as virgins?

An Honorable Father

Many foolish men and women in this fallen world do not value a daughter as highly as they value a son. Although there are various reasons for this trend, I am certain God does not share the prejudice. Frankly, God honors a man when He entrusts him with a daughter. All children need a father's oversight, but a daughter needs that protection more than a son. A daughter may desire and need that protection her entire life if she remains single. How wonderful to see a father cherish his daughter and give her the protection she needs in this sinful world.

Chapter 9

YOUR SON
VS
THE WORLD

Let thy [seed] be blessed:
and rejoice with the wife of thy youth.
Let her be as the loving hind and pleasant roe;
let her breasts satisfy thee at all times;
and be thou ravished always with her love.
Proverbs 5:18-19

We wanted Rick to experience all of the joys of marriage. How were we going to help him maintain moral purity so that he would be qualified to marry a Christian virgin girl?

Preparation for Spiritual Warfare

We knew Rick was headed for spiritual warfare. He would have pressure on him from earliest adulthood to experience immorality, and it could have come even before puberty. Homosexual involvement might be presented to him. His friends might tell about their exploits, whether true or imagined. Neighborhood boys, especially those attending public schools, would not encourage our boy to remain morally chaste.

Therefore, we knew we were the primary positive influence in these matters, unless he was fortunate enough to have a close friend who also had faithful parents. Should our son go away to college or enter the military, he would have tremendous pressure put on him by his peers to throw away his virginity.

We can do all we can to train our son while he is young and pliable, but once he is "on his own" we can only pray. God alone can do what we cannot do. I am a living testimony of God's answer to prayer in this matter. Many of my Christian friends also saved their virginity for their wives. Some of us had our virginity spared *"so as by fire."*

Forgiveness for Failures

A word about those sons who have failed to maintain their virginity: The Bible is a book that convicts us all of sin. No human being has maintained pure righteousness except our Lord. For young men and boys, that is especially true regarding moral purity. God's standard is absolute purity, and we all fall short of His standard. Most, if not all, young men will have committed sexual sins before they marry.

It's good to remember Christ came to redeem sinners, not the good guys. Therefore, if we, our wives, our sons, or our daughters have failed to maintain moral purity even after salvation, we can confess the sins to God and he will forgive us (I John 1:9). Aren't you glad Christ died for all of our sins—past, present, and future?

However, if we sin presumptuously, thinking we can confess our sins and get on with life, we must keep in mind that all sins have consequences. God will not be mocked (See Galatians 6:7).

Pornography

When I was a high school sophomore, we were changing classes one day on the second floor of our school when I noticed a group of boys huddled together. I was curious, so I looked over the shoulder of one fellow to see what the attraction might be.

They were looking at professionally produced "hard core" pornographic comic strips featuring popular cartoon figures. It took only three to four seconds for those images to make an indelible mark on my mind! Praise God for my parental training, especially the

warnings of my dad, that protected me from letting that stuff become a part of my life. I'll discuss more about my parents' training later.

We, you and I, may not have a problem with pornography, but there is a good chance that you, as I did, had some exposure. We also know that as long as we live, we will need God's protection. What an excellent reason to pray, *"and lead us not into temptation, but deliver us from evil."* Our heavenly Father delights to answer such prayers. In these last days before Christ comes for His Church (I Thessalonians 4:14-18) Satan will be looking for prey. *"Be sober, be vigilant; because your adversary the devil, as a roaring lion, walketh about, seeking whom he may devour"* (I Peter 5:8).

It's all in Your Head

It is in the *mind* where the battle rages continually for control of our emotions (our hearts). No wonder Solomon warned, *"Keep thy heart with all diligence; for out of it are the issues of life"* (Proverbs 4:23). Paul knew the mind was where Satan would attack Christ's disciples: *"And be not conformed to this world: but be ye transformed by the renewing of your mind, that ye may prove what is that good, and acceptable, and perfect, will of God"* (Romans 12:2 emphasis added).

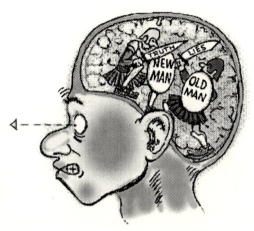

Jesus was referring to the "heart" as a vessel when he said that a person who believes in him will have "living water" flowing out of his inner being (John 7:38). If we are vessels of honor, living water of honorable speech and actions will flow freely from us.

A corrupted person has a corrupted mind (heart), because the mind is where the spiritual heart is. No man who is morally corrupt is capable of spiritual leadership because out of the abundance of his heart his mouth will speak (Luke 6:45). Therefore, we and our sons must avoid pornography like the plague. Hopefully, your son will not fall prey to this horrible trap, and your daughter will not marry a man who is "hooked."

As a vessel of honor, your son or future son-in-law will be qualified and motivated to marry honorably.

Porn and the Pulpit

A few years ago, I learned that several men at a pastor's prayer retreat confessed that they were "hooked" on pornography. As I recall, one of the men asked for prayer for deliverance from this problem. The leader of the group asked if there were others experiencing the same problem. One third of the group raised their hands, some immediately, and others more slowly.

It was sobering to learn that so many spiritual leaders of congregations fell prey to this temptation. These men had given their lives to full-time service for our Lord, but some had allowed their minds to become vessels of dishonor—chamber pots, if you will! If that happened to these men, it is certain that many other Christian men are also hooked on pornography.

Sexual sins like pornography and fornication will damage or destroy potential spiritual leadership. We must warn our sons about this danger before they enter puberty. Post-puberty instruction may be too late.

Valuable Virginity

If a young adult man gives his virginity to a girl who is not his wife, wouldn't he carry that first intimate sexual experience with him into his marriage? I've noticed that young fellows who do not value their virginity will often have multiple partners before they marry. This is especially true in this "free love" generation. I am convinced that this may be the reason why many Christian leaders do not have spiritual discernment in this area. It may also be the reason why they are unable to teach others how to live morally pure lives.

If our sons become true disciples of our Lord Jesus Christ, and followers of our devout leadership, they will bring joy and honor to us. They will bless us with principled daughters-in-law, and well-trained grandchildren. I know this to be true. I've seen it happen many times among my missionary colleagues, friends and relatives.

Blessed indeed is the man and his wife whose sons and daughters marry as virgins.

A godly woman added to this by saying, "There are also blessings for the sons and daughters-in-law who obey. Mom and Dad are not the only ones blessed when two virgins marry!"

Womanly Advice

A young mother told me that it seemed to her that I was more concerned about warning girls about young men and not concerned enough about cunning young women. She made it clear that girls can play a crucial role in the destruction of moral purity. Agreeing with her, I modified some of the material in this book because of her counsel. We both recognized there are rebellious daughters with adamic natures who willfully go against God and their parents. This kind of girl, even if she claims to know Christ, may set out to entice a young man to commit fornication with her. Many girls have rebelled and chosen to go the way of a harlot (Cf. Genesis 38:24).

Youthful Joseph, though a slave in Egypt, proved to be a very wise and godly man. He escaped from his master's wife who sought to seduce him. Joseph, like you and me, also had a fallen nature. His was no small temptation—very likely Potiphar's wife was quite attractive, much younger than her  husband, and was required to share Potiphar's affections with several concubines. (Having multiple wives was common then just as it is today in many African, Middle-eastern, and Asian countries.) She lusted for the sexual favors of her husband's slave, but Joseph feared God and ran. She was humiliated. In revenge, she falsely accused Joseph of attempted rape and had her husband throw the youth into prison. However, God was with the Joseph and eventually caused him to become the Prime Minister of Egypt, second only to Pharaoh. (Read this fascinating story in Genesis 39).

Many men have been exposed to sexual temptation but they saw the danger of it and, like Joseph, they ran from it.

Protecting Our Sons

The only way I know to help our sons escape pornographic addiction is:

- Get in the habit of listening to him
- Discuss any issue that is important to him
- Accept him as a man, not a kid
- Address the hard-to-ask questions
- Demonstrate how faithful friends will hold him accountable

When our son reached age thirteen, we began to respect him as a young, but *immature adult*. Furthermore, in order to be successful with Rick I had to be in fellowship with my wife. You see, Rick usually felt more comfortable pouring out his thoughts to his mom. She would then keep me informed and help keep my spiritual antennas sensitive.

A True Disciple

A true disciple is someone who has committed his life to Christ **_after_** receiving the free gift of eternal life (Romans 5:15-19). A faithful disciple has separated himself from the world, and has sanctified himself (I Peter 3:15-16). He refuses to be involved in "uncleanness."

> *"Be ye not unequally yoked together with unbelievers: for what fellowship hath righteousness with unrighteousness? And what communion hath light with darkness? And what concord hath Christ with Belial? Or what part hath he that believeth with an infidel? And what agreement hath the temple of God with idols? For ye are the temple of the living God; as God hath said, I will dwell in them, and walk in them; and I will be their God,*

and they shall be my people. Wherefore come out from among them, and be ye separate, saith the Lord, and touch not the unclean thing; and I will receive you, and will be a Father unto you, and ye shall be my sons and daughters, saith the Lord Almighty" (II Corinthians 6:14-18).

Conclusion

Satan uses pornography to entrap men of all ages. None of us are exempt from this temptation. This horrible form of fornication has even entrapped many Christian leaders. Our sons will escape enslavement to pornography if they truly know Christ and become His disciples. A faithful Christian father or godly male mentor is the secret to helping committed young men become vessels of honor.

Chapter 10

FINDING GOD'S WILL

For this is the will of God, even your sanctification,
that ye should abstain from fornication
(I Thessalonians 4:3)

How do we find God's will for our lives? Well, it is not as difficult as you think. You were probably hoping I'd tell you how to find the right car, job, career, or girl. Let's handle that quickly. Walk in the Spirit and choose the one you like. God's will for you is that you separate yourself (sanctify yourself) from this world and its lusts (I John 2:15-17), and be fully committed to the Lord Jesus Christ.

Sanctified Dating and Courtship

Most disciples of Christ will agree that fornication (sexual immorality) is a violation of God's will. I Thessalonians 4:3-8 tells us where to draw the line when we are out with our girlfriend on a date. Which, of course, we all want to know, right? Well, at least the girls might want to know. We will focus on that subject later.

"Dating," "going out," and "having a relationship" are common terms, but courtship is an older term that carries a higher degree of commitment. Courting was something great-great grandparents used to do before Hollywood's lustful wrestling became the norm. Courting was a period of time when an honorable young man and a virtuous young woman determined whether God would be pleased if they pursued marriage. It was during courtship that a couple would discern if they were spiritually compatible.

The Bible does not mention courtship. What was practiced in Jesus' day was "betrothal." A young man and woman who were betrothed had already made a formal commitment to marriage.

Yet, they were still under the supervision of their parents. The consummation of the marriage would take place after the wedding ceremony. However, the bridegroom would wait until he had prepared a place for his bride, and then he would come for her when all was in order.

(For an amusing view of betrothal consider reading "To Betroth or Not to Betroth?" by Michael Pearl of No Greater Joy Ministries, 1000 Pearl Road, Pleasantville, TN 37033, <nogreaterjoy.org>).

"Positional" and "Personal" Sanctification

Early in my Christian life, I learned from preachers and Bible teachers that sanctification means "to be set apart for God," and that God sanctifies believers because of Christ's sacrifice for our sins. Bible teachers call that *positional* sanctification. God declares all believers holy when He adopts them into His family the moment they accept Christ as their Savior. That is why Paul addresses all believers as "saints"—holy people, sanctified ones, godly. We don't look holy. Most of us probably do not feel very holy, but God says we are. He says this because we are spiritually *in Christ*, not because we have lived a righteous life.

Another form of sanctification involves something we can do. This kind of sanctification Paul mentions in I Thessalonians 4:3. It begins by declaring it is God's will for us to set ourselves apart for Him.

The Apostle Peter said, *"sanctify the Lord God in your hearts. Be ready always to give an answer to every man that asks you a reason of the hope that is in you with meekness and fear: Having a good conscience; that, whereas they speak evil of you, as of evildoers, they may be ashamed that falsely accuse your good [behavior] in Christ. For it is better, if the will of God be so, that you suffer for well doing, than for evil doing"* (I Peter 3:15-17). You can see that this type of sanctification is connected to our conduct.

I Thessalonians 4:3, however, includes *"that you abstain from fornication."* Now we have something cooking here that needs careful consideration. I think I can clarify this by referring to Abraham.

A Strange Sign

Abram (later Abraham) had been called by God to leave his home country, his dad, mom, and all of his relatives (which incidentally solved a lot of family problems), and go to Canaan where God would re-locate him and his descendants permanently.

God also told Abram that the Messiah would come through the bloodline of Abram and Sarai's son, even though Sarai (later Sarah) had long since gone through "the change of life" (Genesis 17:17; 18:11-14; 21:12; Hebrews 11:17-18). You can understand why she chuckled derisively at the angel's declaration. What sensible woman past 75 years of age expects to have a nursing infant? Nevertheless, Abram believed God would do what he promised. God was pleased with his faith, and declared Abram righteous.

But Abram got impatient waiting for God's promise, so he listened to Sarai's solution regarding a male heir, which led to Abram's son by Hagar, Sarai's Egyptian servant girl. Hagar's son, Ishmael, became Abram's first-born son, but Ishmael was not the *promised child*. That child had to come through Sarai as God had promised.

Later, God changed Abram and Sarai's names to Abraham and Sarah. It was then that God commanded Abraham to be circumcised as a *sign* of the covenant between them. God also commanded circumcision of all male Hebrews (the name of Abraham's people), all male Hebrew children in succeeding generations, and all male individuals under Hebrew authority.

> *"And God said unto Abraham, You shall keep my covenant therefore, you, and your seed after you in their generations. This is my covenant, which you shall keep, between me and you and your seed after you; every man child among you shall be circumcised. And you shall circumcise the flesh of your foreskin; and it*

shall be a token of the covenant between me and you. And he that is eight days old shall be circumcised among you, every man child in your generations, he that is born in the house, or bought with money of any stranger, which is not of your seed. He that is born in your house, and he that is bought with your money, must [of necessity] be circumcised: and my covenant shall be in your flesh for an everlasting covenant. And the uncircumcised man child whose flesh of his foreskin is not circumcised, that soul shall be cut off from his people; he hath broken my covenant" (Genesis 17:9-14).

Abraham and Sarah were ready to produce Isaac *after* God gave that sign. You might say then, that Isaac, God's choice to be heir, *passed through the sign of the covenant.*

What a strange sign! And why put the sign...uh...there?! And it was a gender discrimination sign—men only! What about the women? Why didn't they get a special sign, too?

We will cover the women's part in this matter, but let us deal with the men first.

It seems that circumcision was God's way of separating the Hebrews from all of the other people in the world. Circumcision was not a common practice in those days. Since God had given authority to men over their households, it was they who bore the sign.

God had led Abraham to a land called Canaan, which was dominated by licentious pagan cultures and religions. The Canaanites and other peoples living in the same region (Hittites, Perrizzites, Jebusites, etc.) had temples for their idols in which there were male and female prostitutes who "ministered" to the worshippers. It was expected of everyone to be involved in this socially and politically correct "spiritual" activity.

Now, imagine a young Hebrew man who desired acceptance in this new land—you know, "do as the Hittites do," so to speak.

He undresses in preparation for the ceremonies. Eyes of the priests and priestesses bulge, and exclamations burst out. "Hey, what is this with you, man! You're really different!"

The Hebrew smiles a sick, self-conscious smile and attempts an explanation—"Uh, yeah, uh, well, you see, that's a sign of our God."

"Just who is this god? That's one weird sign if you ask me!"

"Yeah, I guess you're right about that. His name is... Uhm... Maybe I'll just get dressed. It doesn't seem like I fit in here very well."

"No, you don't fit in at all! Your God is really different!"

Yes, the Hebrew's God and His people were set apart from the rest of the world. The physical act of circumcision sanctified the Hebrew men. It was required, and it was a symbol of their obedience to God. Those who refused circumcision for themselves or for their children were to be "cut off"—executed. God wanted His chosen men to have a sign on their bodies in a place where it would make a major difference—to "separate the sheep from the goats."

What about the Hebrew Ladies?

As we know, God has sanctified the virgin, to some extent, by providing her a hymen. It seems that no other sign of physical sanctification was necessary for the Hebrew women since they were apparently under the protection of men, both physically and spiritually. If the men behaved responsibly, then the women were quite secure. The women's freedom of activity was limited because of this protective authority. The daughter would eventually leave the security of her father and mother's home when she married— the father having received the "bride-price" from the groom. The daughter then came under the protection of her husband.

Rebekah's family practiced this security for her when Abraham, through his trusted servant, acquired Rebekah for Isaac (Genesis 24). We see it again when Jacob purchased Rachel by working seven years for her father Laban (Genesis 29). A bride became the property of her husband after he paid the asking price. The girl was apparently involved in the decision (Genesis 24:58).

The children were also the father's property (Cp. Genesis 31:43). Once the boys became responsible men, however, they were free to take wives and establish families of their own. *"Therefore shall a man leave his father and his mother, and shall cleave unto his wife: and they shall be one flesh"* (Genesis 2:24).

Men were expected to be responsible for those under their authority. It was an ideal program for establishing a secure patriarchal family, and this structure was carried over into the New Testament. God, through the Apostle Paul in I Corinthians 11:3-12 and I Timothy 2:11-14 gave instruction on the order for domestic authority. He did not say women were inferior to men, which, of course, they are not.

God's Plan to Execute Moses

The LORD God was so serious about circumcision that He demanded the execution of any Hebrew male who would not have this sign on his body! Consider God's anger against Moses when Moses failed to circumcise his son. I suspect that his Midianite wife, Zipporah, had discouraged Moses from being faithful to

God's command to sanctify his son by placing this sign on their son's body.

"And it came to pass by the way in the inn, that the LORD met him, and sought to kill him. Then Zipporah took a sharp stone, and cut off the foreskin of her son, and cast it at his feet, and said, Surely a bloody husband art thou to me. So he let him go: then she said, A bloody husband thou art, because of the circumcision" (Exodus 4:24-26).

Here we have Moses, the man chosen by God for the supernatural assignment of leading Israel out of slavery, facing execution by God Himself! Zipporah may not have understood the purpose for circumcision. For sure, she did not appreciate the required surgery.

Circumcision of the Heart

Our Lord is just as serious today about our personal sanctification as the LORD God of Israel was concerned about the sanctification of the Hebrews. He wants us set apart for Him alone because so much is at stake. Our brides, children, grandchildren, great-grandchildren, and our personal influence for Christ are all affected. Our commitment to Christ and moral cleanness separates us from our unbelieving neighbors and the lifestyle they consider normal.

There is a good reason why this chapter focuses on boys and men. If our young Christian men are "circumcised of heart," they will reserve themselves for wives of God's choice and avoid giving affection to someone to whom they are not married. The sensual activity practiced by teenagers and young men who are "dating around"—or whatever it is called in different social circles—is pre-marital preparation for the "marry-go-round" of divorce and re-marriage. We want our young people to avoid such experiences.

"In whom also you are circumcised with the circumcision made without hands. [You have put] off

the body of the sins of the flesh by the circumcision of Christ" (Colossians 2:11).

Pop Porn vs. God's Men

Whom do you think is being targeted by the majority of sensual movies and television programs? It's primarily men and boys, and especially fathers. Without a doubt, the enemy of our souls plays a role in these productions, but our fleshly nature willingly submits to him. Natural mankind of nearly all cultures seems to accept and to accommodate the perversion of God's design.

Our Heavenly Father will have nothing to do with the practice of fornication. Such behavior is an antithesis of what He desires for His people, therefore Christian *disciples* testify to the holiness of our God through moral purity.

It is in the area of our sexuality that we, as God's chosen people, are set apart unto Him. We are no longer unclean. We cannot therefore be complacent regarding our behavior and the training of our children. We must be self-controlled, responsible fathers and husbands so the world can see us as "light and salt." These two Scriptures below are for true disciples who want everyone to know our Lord Jesus Christ:

"Let your light so shine before men, that they may see your good works, and glorify your Father which is in heaven" (Matthew 5:16).

"Follow peace with all men, and holiness, without which no man shall see the Lord..." (Hebrews 12:14).

The way we Christians live our lives clearly affects those around us. Moral purity is expected of us by those who know we are Christ's disciples (See Romans 2:14-16).

Chapter 11

A VESSEL OF HONOR OR JUST A POT

Every one of you should know how to possess his vessel
in sanctification and honor
I Thessalonians 4:4

Pastor Schmitt and Mr. Jones

Several years ago Pastor and Mrs. Schmitt sent their lovely daughter, Mary, off to a Christian college thinking she would probably return one day with a handsome Christian fiancé. The preacher did not seem to realize that his daughter was very vulnerable and needed his pastoral skills more than anyone in his congregation and took little interest in what was happening to her socially. Likewise, Mrs. Schmitt seemed oblivious to the seriousness of her daughters' vulnerability. To her parents, Mary Schmitt at eighteen was an independent adult woman, capable of making her own decisions. The Schmitts had not taken into account the confusion that reigns in the hearts of immature Christian men, even those with honorable intentions. Soon, Mary was involved with a sincere young Christian man whom she hoped to marry. Within a few months, they were engaged.

However, the young man was not emotionally or financially prepared for the responsibilities of marriage. The following week, he broke off the engagement. Mary was devastated. It had all been so beautiful; she had responded to this handsome man's embraces with eager anticipation of marriage and children, but in a brief emotional statement, he brought cruel disillusionment. In such a short time her romantic dream had evaporated and was replaced with the bitter agony of a broken heart.

To make matters worse, they continued to see each other. Now a commitment to marriage was not part of the relationship. Mary needed her father, but he was not there for her. He was too consumed with his spiritual flock to care for his own little lamb. She had her mother, but Mom could not give her the help she needed most. Fortunately, Mary was able to maintain her virginity although with serious difficulty.

Sunday school superintendent Mr. Jeff Jones sincerely loved God and his family. Mr. Jones encouraged his son Kevin to get the Christian education that he had been unable to pursue. Therefore, Kevin set out for college with two primary objectives in mind: find a fiancé who would make a good wife, and discover God's will concerning a career.

Kevin was hoping God would "call" him into the ministry. He was a committed Christian, but one who had a limited understanding of the Scriptures and practical holiness. His church taught him to oppose dancing, drinking, smoking, and going to the movies, but without explanations other than, "They are worldly!" However, Kevin was addicted to TV, and that problem seriously affected his grade point average.

While in high school, Kevin had learned how to win a girl's heart and demonstrate his affection without violating the girl's standards. His church had taught him that fornication and "petting" were wrong, so he accepted a subjective standard of hands-off certain sensitive areas when embracing.

It was immature Kevin who had found Mary, broke her heart, and his own at the same time. In frustration, he joined the military, leaving behind a vulnerable Mary.

Kevin was in serious need of his dad's counsel, but Mr. Jones found communicating with his children difficult. Kevin also needed Pastor Schmitt's advice and consent regarding the courtship of Mary. Pastor Schmitt could have held the young man accountable, but the pastor lacked resolve and possibly the wisdom to protect Mary's spiritual life and emotions.

Dad's Duty

The dads referred to above failed to prepare their children for one of the most critical times of life—that of finding a spouse. They also failed to provide the protection both young people, especially Mary, needed.

We cannot be passive regarding our single adult children who go off to college, Bible school, or into the work place. They might need our counsel and protection at that stage of their lives as much as, if not more than, any other time. Just one unwholesome sexual relationship would be enough to make your son or daughter a vessel of dishonor.

Vessels of Honor

"But in a great house there are not only vessels of gold and of silver, but also of wood and of earth; and some to honour, and some to dishonour. If a man therefore purge himself from these, he shall be a vessel unto honour, sanctified, and meet for the master's use, and prepared unto every good work. Flee also youthful lusts: but follow righteousness, faith, charity, peace, with them that call on the Lord out of a pure heart" (II Timothy 2:20-22).

Fathers, if we are going to protect our daughters and sons from messing up their lives, we must set the example by being vessels of honor ourselves. If you are just a chamber pot morally, then you must take care of that problem immediately. Here are some things you can do to clean up:

- Immediately confess the sins to the Lord (I John 1:9)
- Turn away from whatever immoral thing you are doing—viewing the wrong programs on TV, in movies, magazines, internet, or whatever is corrupting to your character (II Timothy 2:22)
- Let your wife hold you accountable (Genesis 2:18)

- Get your wife's counsel regarding what would be appropriate to confess to your children if they know you are compromised (Genesis 2:18)
- Commit your body and mind to Christ (Romans 12:1-2)

Bold as Lions

Assuming we are now living an honorable, moral life that brings glory to God, we are ready to protect and lead our children. We are qualified to check out the young fellows who have their eyes on our daughters. We are also able to discuss with our sons what a godly man does to find and court a godly young woman. With a conscience clear before God and man, we will be "bold as lions." Proverbs 28:1 says, *"The wicked flee when no man pursueth: but the righteous are bold as a lion."*

Need a Dad and Mom?

Several years ago, Wayne Russell came to visit our niece, Pamela. Wayne was a tall, handsome, broad-shouldered Chico State student with a neat little mustache who, we discovered later, was majoring in secondary education. Pamela's parents were working overseas at the time, so she was living with us until she could make it on her own. She was nineteen, attractive, and vivacious. Wayne was about twenty-one. Pamela had been in our home for about two weeks, so you can understand why I thought to myself, *It sure didn't take long for her to get a fellow's attention.*

After a brief introduction, Pamela and Shirley went to the kitchen to chat, and I invited Wayne to visit with me in our living room. We had not given Pamela an orientation on our policies regarding dating, but we hoped that she had had some training from her parents.

My experience as a father and educator has produced in me an early warning system whenever I sense social complexities beginning to develop. Therefore, I thought it would be prudent to let Wayne know that we have some guidelines that might interest him—you know, sort of lay my cards on the table. Therefore, after a few social pleasantries and background information, I directed the conversation to what was uppermost on my mind—*just how serious was Wayne about Pamela?* I took the direct approach.

"Wayne, Shirley and I wouldn't know, of course, how interested you are in Pamela, but should you desire to begin a relationship with her, we have some guidelines we'd like you to consider."

Wayne was interested immediately in what I had to say, so I began relating some of the principles you've been reading about in this book. As it turned out, Wayne never did begin a serious relationship with Pamela. However, he continued to come over to our home quite frequently for several years.

One day I asked, "Wayne, why is it that you keep coming over to our house and spending time shooting the breeze with me?"

"Bill, I've never met a man who protected his daughters spiritually regarding dating before. That's why I came back. I wanted to know what kind of father would do that. Also, you answered my questions using the Bible." (Opinions and ideas were also expressed, but we made a distinction between those and God's Word.)

One day Wayne related how on two different occasions he had started a dating relationship. Both of these girls had been involved in some form of spiritual leadership at the college or church. However, Wayne quickly stopped dating these girls when he discovered that they expected to be involved sensually with him. This frustrated Wayne because he was hoping to find a girl who desired to follow biblical principles during courtship. Courtship and marriage had become serious matters to Wayne, and he wanted God's blessing on his future family.

Wayne decided to take a short-term mission trip to South America that Shirley and I were leading. Shortly before the time to leave, Wayne met Sharon—a girl attending his home church. It didn't take long for Wayne to realize that Sharon had all of the qualities he was looking for. But what a time to fall in love! He was about to leave for the jungles of Bolivia for six long weeks where he would live in an isolated tribal setting.

During orientation, Wayne found a way to communicate with Sharon—a public telephone. Poor Wayne had it bad. It cost him many dollars in phone calls to curb an insatiable desire to communicate with this lovely woman. When Wayne got to the tribal base deep in the heart of the Amazon Basin he wrote stacks of letters. I suspect he sent and received more letters than our combined team of twenty-six. Obviously, the desire to communicate was as strong in Sharon as it was for Wayne. Oh, what a day it was when Wayne returned from his missions trip!

Their love increased, and so did Wayne's natural hunger, if you know what I mean. He felt he needed help to keep on the straight and narrow, so he gave me a call.

"Bill, Sharon is so desirable! I want to take her in my arms. You know what I mean? But I want to please the Lord. The temptations are so great!"

"Are you and Sharon meeting alone together behind closed doors?"

"Well, yeah. I guess we shouldn't do that, right?"

"It's not a good idea if you want to avoid serious temptation."

"Thanks, Bill."

"You probably shouldn't park your car and talk either."

"Right. We've done that. We'll stop doing it."

It seems that Wayne and Sharon were able to keep themselves reined in pretty well, but then the temptation would become intense again.

"Hi, Bill. Wayne here. I'm finding it really hard again. Got any ideas?" Wayne explained how much he loved Sharon and wanted to honor the Lord in their courtship, but he was afraid he would fail because his desire for her was so great.

"Wayne, can you and Sharon meet us at Denny's for coffee?"

"Sure. Let's do it."

So Shirley and I met with Wayne and Sharon at Denny's restaurant. Following some small talk, we got down to business. Finally, I said, "You know, Sharon's parents are not able to help her. Her dad and mother divorced, and her stepfather is not much help spiritually. Her dad is not a Christian. She really needs Christian parents who could protect her. Sharon, would you mind if Shirley and I adopted you into our family until you and Wayne get married?"

Sharon did not hesitate. She said, "Oh, I'd like that!"

I said, "O.K. Let's raise our cups. Sharon, Shirley and I declare that you are (clink!) adopted into our family as our daughter."

Then I turned to Wayne and said, "Wayne, I want you to keep your prune pick'n patties off our daughter! O.K.?" We all had a laugh, but we knew it was serious business. Shirley and I intended to protect Sharon as best we could, and at the same time protect Wayne too.

Wayne said that this worked for a while, but when he and Sharon were just three months away from their wedding day, he called again.

Bill, the temptation is almost more than I can bear again. Do you have any other ideas?"

"The only thing I can think of is a vow. You can make a solemn vow before God and Sharon that you will not touch her inappropriately until you are married. God will hold you accountable to that vow."

"I'm going to do it, Bill. I have to do something."

"It's a very serious thing to make a vow to God, Wayne. You'd better read Ecclesiastes 5:4-6 first."

That's what Wayne did, and then he said, "I'm going to do it, Bill. I know how serious it is, but I'm desperate."

Wayne made that vow to God before Sharon. After making the vow Sharon said, "Since you made that vow, I'm making it too." And she did.

Some time later Wayne told me that after making the vows they had no more temptation to violate God's standards. They had three months free of temptation!

When they had their wedding, it was one of the most Christ-honoring weddings I have ever witnessed.

Bachelors and Eligible Ladies

If you are an eligible young bachelor looking for a wife, and you have no dad to help you, then you might benefit from this message. Should you be a daughter peeking in on a man's book, hopefully this will be a help to you, too. At least you will know what God expects of us men. Whether you are a bachelor or an eligible woman, I would encourage you to seek and find a godly, mature Christian couple who holds to these convictions to be among your mentors.

Dignity and Honor

"A good name is rather to be chosen than great riches, and loving favour rather than silver and gold" (Proverbs 22:1).

Dads must be convinced that dignity, honor, and love in marriage are destroyed by lust and fornication. Our job is to train children, from the cradle to adulthood, to pursue these three character qualities. It is either God's way with dignity, or Satan's way with dishonor and guilt.

Conclusion

We want our sons and daughters to be of the highest quality when the time comes for marriage. I hope that they will be "vessels of honor." If Dad and Mom are people with good reputations, then the children will probably have good reputations, too. Shirley and I were fortunate to have parents like that. Their reputations made it possible for us to enter places of honor simply because our dads and mothers were honorable. That gave us a significant advantage in a difficult world where people must prudently evaluate each other because of our fallen nature.

However, if your parents are not vessels of honor, God has disciples looking for faithful people. They will gladly invest their lives in you.

Chapter 12

FINDING VESSELS OF HONOR

Look not on his countenance, or on the height of his stature;
because I have refused him: for the LORD seeth not as man
seeth; for man looketh on the outward appearance, but the LORD
looketh on the heart
I Samuel 16:7

A Good Deal or a "Lemon"?

Our Sandi was in need of an immaculate used car in mint condition that got good mpg, had a/c, p/l, p/w, tilt, c/c, s/c, with plenty of h/p and pretty! She sought and got the combined input of her brother and her brother-in-law, a variety of advisers, internet printouts, hours of debate, and multiple test-drives of potential candidates. She finally gained approval on one car from the counselors she trusted most in making her final decision. It was a fantastic buy, but not perfect.

In the process of making this expensive cash investment, I would occasionally comment how buying a car had similarities to getting married. Well, Sandi is now owner of her chosen chariot, affectionately called "Annie," for better or for worse. Fortunately, if the machine turns out to be a "lemon" and doesn't come up to expectations, there will be no problem with starting the process over again.

However, a God-honoring marriage does not enjoy that option (starting over) even when the hidden flaws in a spouse threaten to turn the relationship sour.

Since Rick and I gave counsel and protection to Sandi in purchasing a car, wouldn't it be even more important that we (Rick, her mother and I) help Sandi evaluate potential suitors if she desires our participation? I believe God delights in family unity, and when the family works together wonderful things can happen, including a good marriage (with some exceptions of course).

Any employer would want to know the background experiences, qualifications, and personality characteristics of a potential employee before hiring him/her. He would even want character references from the person's previous employers. How much more important it is for our family to know the person who hopes to marry our son or daughter and parent our grandchildren?

Practical Principles

Various fellows have entered into Sandi's life since her graduation from college several years ago. She has permitted me to write some of the principles she has learned to follow when a fellow takes an interest in her, and there continues to be young men who are still showing interest. As you might suspect, as she gets older and wiser, so do the potential candidates for courtship. With age, though, sometimes comes men who have had a variety of unwholesome experiences of which premarital sex would be only one. Even though we know that God forgives and restores to fellowship those who fall into sin, nevertheless, consequences always follow iniquity. Sandi then must take into account how much collateral damage has happened in the life of a fellow who would consider her a potential bride. Therefore, she attempts to practice the following and stay open to her family's input:

- **Listen to what he says.** It is written that out of the abundance of the heart the mouth speaks (Cp. Matthew 12:34-35). *"For as [a man] thinks in his heart, so is he"* (Proverbs 23:7a). She learns quite a bit about a person when she considers what he says and how he says it.

- **Observe his personal habits**—how he grooms his hair, walks, cares for his shoes and possessions, and personal hygiene. One of the reasons we chose the car we did for Sandi was the neat appearance of the girl who sold it to her, and how she polished and maintained the car. *"Even a child is known by his doings, whether his work be pure, and whether it be right"* (Proverbs 20:11).

- **Know what kind of entertainment he enjoys.** The kind of entertainment a person desires often reflects how dedicated to Christ he may be. If someone loves ungodly entertainment, it may indicate a lack of true faith in Christ. *"If any man love the world, the love of the Father is not in him"* (1 John 2:15).

- **Know what his attitude is toward his parents.** If a candidate is not respectful toward his mother and/or father (Ephesians 6:2-3), he will bring that character flaw into a marriage. What you see is what you will get. An insensitive son will be an insensitive spouse.

- **Meet his parents and learn how they relate with their son.** Children will bring many family characteristics of the parents into their marriage. Our parents influence us more than we realize. *"For I know [Abraham], that he will command his children and his household after him, and they shall keep the way of the LORD, to do justice and judgment; that the LORD may bring upon Abraham that which he hath spoken of him"* (Genesis 18:19).

- **Learn what his parents believe.** Parents' philosophical convictions are usually passed on to their children. Ask yourself, *Do his Christian parents believe the Bible regarding the discipline of children?* Paul wrote to Timothy,

"When I call to remembrance the unfeigned faith that is in thee, which dwelt first in thy grandmother Lois, and thy mother Eunice; and I am persuaded that in thee also" (2 Timothy 1:5).

I am sure we could add to this list, but Sandi also has to keep in mind that she cannot find a perfect mate with perfect parents any more than she could find a perfect car.

Being single can be heavenly compared to some marriages. Do you remember Peter's response when Jesus taught the disciples regarding divorce and remarriage?

The "Adamic factor" has affected us all, but there are some sins that have greater consequences than others. Perhaps that is one of the reasons Paul wrote, *"Art thou bound unto a wife? Seek not to be loosed. Art thou loosed from a wife? Seek not a wife. But and if thou marry, thou hast not sinned; and if a virgin marry, she hath not sinned. Nevertheless such shall have trouble in the flesh: but I spare you"* (Corinthians 7:27-28 emphasis added).

God's Transforming Power

We know that any person could be renewed spiritually and become a vessel of honor. Through Christ, the sinful heart of man can be cleansed and regenerated. Consider adulterous King David's cry of repentance in Psalm 51:10: *"Create in me a clean heart, O God; and renew a right spirit within me."*

This raises a heavy-duty question. Is there hope for a godly marriage if a son has sacrificed his virginity? Yes. However, there must be no assumption that he has a right to marry a virgin if he is not a virgin himself. God does renew a right spirit in one who sins, but the consequences still follow. Again, God is not mocked, and what a person sows produces serious fall-out (Galatians 6:7). Consider the severe consequences King David of Israel had following his sin with Bathsheba—the death of the baby, the rape of his daughter by David's son, the murder of that son, and the rebellion and assassination of his beloved Absalom who led a coup against David. Yet God loved David and considered him *"a man after [His] own heart"* (Acts 13:22).

Satan's Primary Targets

Some years ago there was a popular Christian book entitled "Point Man" by Steve Farrar. This author demonstrated why Dad is the primary target of Satan—like the "point man" that leads his platoon into combat. He said the devil targets the number one guy in the family, and Farrar is right! The devil knows well how effective dads can be, and the devil does not fight fair. If Satan messes Dad up through deceit, then the whole family is in serious trouble!

Satan goes for the head, the one that has authority from God to set standards. The reason for this spiritual assault by our ancient enemy is the role men are designed to play in this fantastic plan of God. Satan knows that discipleship is the most dangerous offensive Christ has given the Church (Cp. Matthew 28:18-20).

The devil is very concerned about women discipling women and girls, but he gets especially disturbed, I believe, when someone disciples a member of the male gender. Satan targets little boys, teenage boys, young men, as well as fathers, and maybe single men even more than the rest. Most boys and young men will become heads of households. Doesn't Satan also target girls and young women? Certainly, but they are secondary targets who might be used to damage a primary target (Cp. Proverbs 14:1).

Yes, you are the primary target, Dad, and your wife and children are the secondary targets. We dads are the heads of our homes, and our sons will be the heads of their homes. If our dignity and honor has been tarnished, our entire family will be affected. It may appear that Mom or the kids are the primary targets at times, but our enemy may be getting at Dad through one or more of them.

The Bible has clearly set up an order of authority starting with God the Father, then Christ, then Dad, then Mom, and finally the kids. *"But I would have you know, that the head of every man is Christ; and the head of the woman is the man; and the head of Christ is God"* (1 Corinthians 11:3).

Satan's Arsenal

It has helped our children for us to ask the following questions. Do most children in the Western World love and respect their fathers after they enter their teens? No. Do American sitcoms portray Dad as honorable and wise? No, Father is portrayed as a foolish guy who needs constant correction by his wife and kids. Even the "heroes" in entertainment productions behave like fools when they are viewed in the light of God's Word. Who enjoys American football on Sunday and Monday nights, Mom or Dad? Dad does, because football is a man's type of sport. Ever wonder why seductively clad women are used to advertise beer?—because it motivates Mom to buy a six-pack at the first opportunity, right? Of course not. We know Dad's the target. Booze and lust can contribute to his becoming a lousy example to his family. If Dad is discredited as the number one authority in the home and if he is irresponsible in his pleasures, the wife and kids lose their most vital spiritual authority.

It is not enough for Mom to be a good person and set an example. She's limited in her authority, even though her  influence is powerful and essential. However, if Satan (See Revelation 12:3) draws Dad into foolishness, the family will be seriously weakened spiritually and emotionally. Therefore, one of Satan's primary objectives is to discredit Dad and destroy his credibility as the head of his home. Satan is depicted in Revelation as a seven headed dragon.

I have no doubt that it is God's desire that we dads become powerful influences and effective protectors—bold as lions! Not only is it His desire for us, but He has given us all we need to be the best dads we can be (Cf. II Peter 1:3-8). His Spirit will motivate us to obey His Word (Ephesians 5:8-10) so that we can avoid sin and act wisely (Psalm 119:9-11; Proverbs 2:5-7).

Real Repentance

My Christian dad was about thirty-six when he came to repentance for living a self-willed life. He and my mother had received Christ in their youth, but his lack of commitment had taken a spiritual toll on our little family of four: Dad, Mom, Ken, and me. Mom was faithful, and Ken had assurance of his salvation, but I was confused. I have no idea what Dad was doing, but whatever it was, he knew God was not pleased with him. I will never forget how Dad came under conviction during an "old fashioned revival" service at our church. He nearly ran to the front of the auditorium and fell on his knees at the "mourner's bench." I was thirteen at the time. From then on, Dad was the spiritual head of our home and a faithful witness. Three years after Dad's renewal experience, I accepted Christ as my Savior at a Youth for Christ rally. Furthermore, Dad's faithfulness set a high standard of discipleship for my brother and me.

Conclusion

An honorable dad, as head of his home, is the key person in preparing his children to marry "vessels of honor." However, that dad must be a vessel unto honor, not a chamber pot.

Chapter 13

GOD'S GIFT TO ADAM

*This is now bone of my bones, and flesh of my flesh: she shall be
called Woman, because she was taken out of Man*
Genesis 2:23

Adam's most cherished gift from God was Eve, of course. He even
loved her more than he loved God or his own life. Nevertheless,
God still loved Adam and Eve in spite of their sins. He also loves
us, their descendants, in spite of *our* sins. Therefore, Shirley and I
taught our children that God has revealed ways for the descendents
of Adam and Eve to have wonderful pleasures in spite of The Fall.
Perhaps one of the greatest of these pleasures is romance!

A Return to Eden

It is the middle of a late spring evening in Northern California.
Snowcapped mountains are silhouetted beyond the shores of a lake

that reflects a silvery path of light from a full moon just above the horizon. Ben and Ruth are sitting close together in Ben's sporty convertible with the top down. We can see their heads together in gentle intimacy as they gaze upon the God-given scene before them. As Ben puts his arm around Ruth, she snuggles into that special indentation below his shoulder that was designed in Adam as a nestling place for Eve.

Ruth prepared herself with great care for this moment. Within such close proximity, Ben could detect the delicate fragrance of perfume and a touch of color on her lips and cheeks. She is dressed in a simple white blouse with a modestly opened collar revealing a delicate gold chain that accents her graceful neck. Ruth is serene with pleasure and a sense of security.

The moisture in her eyes catches the moon's light as she surveys her companion's handsome face. Ben is clean-shaven, bathed, "deodorized," brushed, and dressed carefully in matching shirt, pants, and socks. He has a slight Colgate flavor in his mouth and a touch of after-shave lotion on his smooth, youthful cheeks. Ben's body is in excellent health and vibrating with desire. He surveys the delightful features of this creature resting on his chest.

Ben is tormented with passion, and like his ancestor, Adam, exclaims within himself to God, "Oh, Lord! This is it! Wow! What a creature! And she's all mine!" He can no longer hold back the impulse to place his eager lips upon those that are made irresistible in the illumination of the lights of the heavens. She eagerly awaits his advances with equal anticipation and desire.

Ben and Ruth's wedding ceremony earlier that day had been a beautiful and well-planned event. The church had been full of friends and relatives. But the joy of that occasion could not compare to the ecstasy of this, their moment of innocent intimacy. They are eager to drink deeply, for the first time, of this God created pleasure that is now legitimately theirs.

"Let thy fountain [sperm or children] be blessed: and rejoice with the wife of thy youth. Let

her be as the loving hind and pleasant roe; let her breasts satisfy thee at all times; and be thou ravished always with her love" (Proverbs 5:18-19).

Only One Eve

Can we not agree with all idealists everywhere that the attraction for the opposite sex is compelling and may be exquisitely beautiful, especially if it is seasoned with unselfish love? Because God is the author of such intimacy (Genesis 2:20 ff.), it was designed to be wonderful. Therefore, a young couple may drink deeply and often from this well of pleasure beginning the very night after they make their solemn vows of loyalty and devotion to each other before God and man. In fact, it is an honorable practice that God encourages (See Hebrews 13:4; Cp. I Corinthians 7:2-4).

Indeed, it was God who designed young men and women to be highly motivated to carry out his command to be fruitful and multiply.

> *Thou hast ravished my heart, my sister, my spouse.*
> *How fair is thy love, my sister, my spouse!*
> *How much better is thy love than wine!*
> (From Song 4:9-10)
> *His mouth is most sweet:*
> *yea, he is altogether lovely.*
> *This is my beloved,*
> *and this is my friend*
> (From Song 5:16)

Day Dreams and Reality

I remember my pre-puberty days when I dreamed of the faceless girl that would eventually become my bride and mother of my children. Looking back at these daydreams has given birth to a theory that borders on conviction; I believe God has placed in the heart of every boy the desire for one girl—the girl of his dreams. My wife tells me that God has planted the same desire in the hearts of girls. In my primary school days, so many girls seemed to be possibilities. Each Valentines Day found me actively searching for the appropriate card for the special girl that had my interest at that particular moment. By the time I was in the fourth grade, though, I had become more realistic. Despite the fact that Valentines Day was encouraged  by the public school system, some girls simply did not want my valentines, or they wanted valentines from someone else. No big deal, though—there were plenty of other possibilities, and I was learning some important lessons regarding the fickleness of the human heart, including my own.

When I reached early adolescence, a subtle chemical change affected my perspective. I became aware of a tiger of passion in me that I had not known before. The ideals were still there, but they were clouded by this new development. I knew I had to control it, or it would control me, so began an intense spiritual battle to maintain chastity.

In the early stages of manhood (about 13) I was spiritually, emotionally, and physically at war with a force that was greater than I was. I'm not talking about demons. I'm talking about what the King James Version of the Bible calls "the flesh." This "flesh" is the appetite for unwholesome pleasure that I inherited from my forefather, Adam. After nearly seven years of bruising warfare, it helped to realize that God had originally designed man this way, but without a sin nature to mess things up. (Incidentally, university psychology teachers presented to me the foolish notion that these conflicts of the soul were examples of mental disorders generated by overly strict parents and religious leaders.)

Sound doctrine eventually made clear that I was a normal product of Adam's fallen race, and that there was wisdom in the Bible that deals with this passion problem.

Adam's Fallen Flesh

After The Fall, Adam had some major difficulties that were passed on primarily to men and boys. We men have reproduction chemistry flowing through our bodies that was designed for a perfect person—Adam before he sinned. Adam was morally pure when he received his reproductive features, but his fallen nature— the flesh that we inherited—makes demands that are impossible to satisfy. This problem became evident before I had the wisdom, knowledge, and understanding that come only by revelation from God's Word. Because I experienced some rough sledding, I'm usually empathetic when I hear about problems affecting other members of my gender.

Missing the Golden Experience

It does not surprise me that the method of seeking and finding a suitable spouse is generally perverted in non-Christian societies. All cultures in this world corrupt that golden experience where a man and his wife become truly one in a spiritual sense. Missionaries have long known that most cultures accept perversions as normal. As our American culture moves farther from its Christian heritage, the more distorted will be our relationships with the opposite sex.

There is only one hope for a significant measure of the original experiences that were Adam and Eve's before their sin. Christians who are spiritually "born again" can escape the tyranny of Adam's nature. *"For sin shall not have dominion over you: for ye are not under the law, but under grace."* (Romans 6:14). But how does grace work? It helps to understand just who we are now that we are *in* Christ and *out* of Adam. More on this later.

More Precious than Rubies

"Who can find a virtuous woman? for her price is far above rubies. The heart of her husband doth safely trust in her, so that he shall have no need of spoil. She will do him good and not evil all the days of her life" (Proverbs 31:10-12).

The key word, of course, is virtuous. A virtuous woman is one who has an excellent reputation, is prudent, noble, and morally pure. She is also a person who fears God and loves His Book.

Worldly men seek for that one perfect Eve. When money and power do not fill a void in their lives they theorize that somehow that perfect *Eve* is their ticket to fulfillment, only to be disillusioned. They are seeking that joy God designed for a perfect Adam.

Perhaps in a similar way the Eves of this world are hoping for that special Adam, and so we have a proliferation of unrealistic (or too realistic) romance novels and tabloid farces. The Bible tells it like it is: *"Hell and destruction are never full; so the eyes of man are never satisfied"* (Proverbs 27:20).

Shirley and I have observed that in both primitive and "advanced" cultures 'Adams' and 'Eves' are frustrated and disillusioned. Interpersonal conflicts seem to be the norm in most homes, especially between a husband and wife. It is not surprising that most professional counseling involves family conflicts.

Good News for Christians

Only God's people are the candidates for a truly satisfying marriage in which *"agape"* and *"philanthropia"* love are developed. You may not experience all the blessings Adam had before the Fall, but you will have experiences with your personal 'Eve' that will bless your socks off! God's people have the Scriptures where wisdom, knowledge, and understanding are found. The Bible reveals God's secrets concerning a realistic and delightful marriage.

This is not exclusively for those who are raised in godly Christian homes. The blessing of a God-centered courtship is available to any child of God in spite of the sinful background he may have had before he came to Christ. *Therefore if any man be in Christ, he is a new creature: old things are passed away; behold, all things are become new* (II Corinthians 5:17).

Summary

We cannot fully experience all that Adam had with Eve before The Fall, but God's people can recapture a good measure of that pleasure. Children are born with the longings for the intimacies God gave Adam and Eve, but at puberty, we fellows discover our delightful male kitten has become a hungry tiger. Worldly men fantasize about a golden intimacy but the world usually corrupts what they long for. However, the psalmist wrote this wonderful verse to encourage God's people: *"For the LORD God is a sun and shield: the LORD will give grace and glory: no good thing will he withhold from them that walk uprightly"* (Psalm 84:11 emphasis added).

Chapter 14

COUNTERING CULTURE

*Not in the lust of concupiscence, even as the
Gentiles who know not God
I Thessalonians 4:5*

Shirley and I became concerned about dating and courtship when our older daughters reached the age of puberty. We had observed the consequences of teenage dating relationships for several years as professional secondary teachers. We realized that we might have a major disaster in our family if our daughters started dating.

A seminar that my wife and I attended underscored the convictions that were forming in my mind. This was the first time we heard teaching that challenged the sensual practices of so-called "Christian dating" from a biblical perspective. God used this seminar to reach my lethargic spiritual brain just in time to illustrate how we might help our daughters avoid the pitfalls of dating.

I realized that the accepted Christian standard for premarital conduct fell considerably below the biblical standard. Many Christians may have had a higher standard, but that position was not emphasized in the churches, at youth meetings, or at the Christian colleges I attended. I don't recall any of my pastors, Bible teachers, or youth leaders clearly addressing this important subject of biblical dating, courtship, and marriage.

Bible teachers alluded to the evils of petting, fornication, adultery, and sensual entertainment. However, they did not offer clear biblical guidelines for young Christians involved in dating relationships. Instead the church leaders seem to accept a slightly modified American cultural standard of permissive sensuality. In my observations of Christian young people, most accepted this standard unquestioningly.

When I was in my late teens there was a young couple in my local conservative church hugging and cuddling during the meetings. They were my age—about nineteen. Such open affection during church meetings didn't seem right to me. No one, including the pastor, apparently knew that I Thessalonians 4:3-7 opposed their conduct. Perhaps some people considered their behavior normal and romantic, and some enjoyed gossiping about them. Curiously, the public cuddling stopped after they were married.

After church on Sunday evenings, it was common for several teenagers to pair off, drive around town, then stop at a drive-in restaurant, and later park somewhere and "neck." Looking back, I am convinced that this behavior is a central reason why so many young folks left their local churches after high school and never returned.

Shirley and I were determined to protect our children from this kind of destructive "Christian" culture.

The American Way

With that goal in mind, we began to teach our children that the American way of dating, called *romance,* is the antithesis of God's design, and often encourages fornication. Our children learned that romantic dating can become a vicious cycle of intimacy—"breaking up" and starting another intimate relationship with someone else. They could see that dating and breaking up educates people to accept divorce and remarriage as normal.

No wonder Paul warned the Thessalonians to avoid the "lust of concupiscence" (KJV). I find it interesting that the god of lust, Cupid, is in the middle of the word concupiscence—"con" (with) "cupi" (lust) "scence" (fullness), (See The New American Dictionary). Apparently, the American way was also the Greek and Roman way in Paul's day.

Qualified Christian Leaders

We hoped our daughters would marry godly Christians who were potential spiritual leaders. We also hoped our son would find a prudent wife who would be supportive of his leadership.

They needed to understand how sensual dating could affect a young man who would one day aspire to be a spiritual leader. If he has caressed a variety of girls before marriage, he might disqualify himself from becoming a church officer even if he had never had sexual intercourse with any of them. His experiences could affect his loyalty to the woman he eventually marries. Can a man who is not devoted to his wife be qualified to lead the local church? No. An elder must be the husband of *one* wife—a one-woman-man. *"A bishop [elder, pastor] then must be blameless, the husband of one wife, vigilant, sober, of good behavior..."* (1 Timothy 3:2).

Marriage and the Creation of Life

Shirley and I tried to convince our children that the marriage relationship is much more than friendship, love, oneness, etc. It is even more crucial than a child-parent relationship. But why? Consider this: Two people come together in the most intimate of all activity, and from that delightful pleasure is the potential for the reproduction of life. The woman provides her unique contribution, the man provides his, and from these come a biological miracle that results in a living human being! A new family is fully realized! The child is living testimony of the bond between the father and mother. The future of that child will be affected according to the bond of love between the parents.

The father and mother's parents and extended families cannot be included in what God accomplishes in this blessed event. The man and woman who produce this new human being become one flesh. That creative act is much more than gratifying a physical desire.

A God-fearing man has a realistic hope of a beautiful marriage with his virgin bride that will last till "death do [them] part."

Propaganda

Beware lest any man spoil you through philosophy and vain deceit, after the tradition of men, after the rudiments of the world, and not after Christ" (Colossians 2:8).

As a family, we rejected the social propaganda promoting modern romance. We also boycotted productions that graphically portrayed immorality and/or blasphemed our Lord.

Secular media attempts to portray popular people who have had multiple sexual partners in a positive light. We pointed this out to our children, and let them "know… the rest of the story." *Wherefore come out from among them, and be ye separate, saith the Lord, and touch not the unclean thing; and I will receive you, And will be a Father unto you, and ye shall be my sons and daughters, saith the Lord Almighty* (II Corinthians 6:17-29).

Chapter 15

MACHISMO

That no man go beyond and defraud his brother in any matter:
because that the Lord is the avenger of all such,
as we also have forewarned you and testified
I Thessalonians 4:6

A True *Macho*

When we lived in Bolivia, South America, I knew a *macho* that was top dog in the neighborhood. He was a handsome creature and very jealous of his territory. No one dared to intrude into his domain because to do so was to endanger your life. You might say he ruled all of his subjects, both male and female, with ruthless intolerance, never showing mercy or weakness. He was proud, arrogant, and promiscuous. He masterfully lived up to his nickname "Pepper" because he was spicier than any other creature under his tyranny.

Pepper was our dog—part Irish Setter and part *perro general*, or "mutt" in American English. The Irish Setter in him made him lovable, but the mutt in him kept him up late at night and often in the wrong neighborhood. I assume my dog sought to maintain an impressive image by the way he strutted around the neighborhood in the presence of other members of his species— panting, sniffing, and just being *macho*.

This Spanish word *macho* means male, and is commonly used in Bolivia to distinguish the gender of beasts such as horses, mules, dogs, cats, etc. However, it is also used in America and other countries to describe a man who has irresistible masculine attributes when it comes to sexual conquests. Many young men, and some not so young, are proud of their macho image. A human macho may have even bragged about the number of girls whose virginity he had stolen.

By contrast, the Spanish word for a female animal is *hembra*. In the case of a dog, the equivalent in English would be b—. Certainly, no self-respecting Spanish woman would want to be referred to as an *hembra* just as an honorable English speaking lady would not like to be called a b—. Isn't it interesting that some men like being known as machos? Nevertheless, the word *macho* is generally used in reference to a male beast just as the term *hembra* is recognized as referring to a female beast.

Pepper's natural behavior was perfectly in order for his species, as a dog. He did exactly what God designed a *macho* to do. Pepper's species was not created in God's image; only mankind shares some of God's attributes. Men, though, are not beasts even if they act like it, and *machismo* (beastly behavior), is definitely not a complimentary characteristic for people created in God's image. Perhaps they do not understand that *macho* best describes a beast, not a man created in God's image.

Machismo

Once a youth has decided to "learn the ropes" of *machismo* he will soon discover he has developed a craft that serves an appetite that is impossible to satisfy. He will know how to win a girl, and how to manipulate her. He will learn the art of stimulating physical passions, but he may not care how adversely this may affect the girl's future. He may appear to care (which is part of the deception), but his pursuit of lust will cloud his mind.

Christian *Machismo*

Shirley and I had to warn our daughters that many young "Christian" men have a tendency toward *machismo*, and their number is increasing with the spiritual "falling away" in most American churches.

I have known several Christians over the years that practiced *machismo*. They have broken the hearts of numerous girls and stolen their virginity. Christian parents must be vigilant if they are to protect their daughters from these men.

> *"This know also, that in the last days perilous times shall come. For men shall be lovers of their own selves, covetous, boasters, proud, blasphemers, disobedient to parents, unthankful, unholy, without natural affection, trucebreakers, false accusers, incontinent, fierce, despisers of those that are good, traitors, heady, highminded, lovers of pleasures more than lovers of God. Having a form of godliness, but denying the power thereof. From such turn away"* (II Timothy 3:1-5).

Protecting our Sons

A father and mother can work together to train their son to avoid *machismo* by beginning when he is a small child. However, division in the home may encourage a son to look to his peers for direction. If parents wait until he becomes a teenager, his peers might have greater influence on their son than they have. Dad's role as the father and head of the home and Mom's indispensable support of Dad's authority are critical

The son who begins to practice *machismo* will dishonor his parents and all who love him. He will deprive his bride of the gift of virginity and chastity. *"A foolish son is a grief to his father, and bitterness to her that bare him"* (Proverbs 17:25). As a Christian, he will grieve the Holy Spirit who dwells in him, and he will suffer severe discipline as a child of God. That discipline could result in life-long consequences. *"For whom the Lord loveth he chasteneth, and scourgeth every son whom he receiveth. If ye endure chastening, God dealeth with you as with sons; for what son is he whom the father chasteneth not? But if ye be without chastisement, whereof all are partakers, then are ye bastards, and not sons"* (Hebrews 12:6-8 emphasis added). All true Christians receive God's loving discipline.

Machismo vs. **Daughters**

Bob practiced *machismo* as a student at a Christian high school and seemed to be able to get any girl he desired. He chose Trisha, one of the most attractive. Bob's supervisor, Mr. George Rice, knew about Bob's reputation with the girls, so he kept a close eye on him. Mr. Rice also knew it would be impossible to know what Bob and Trisha were doing twenty-four hours a day. His years of experience with teenage boys led him to seek out Trisha's father to see if something could be done to protect the girl. Trisha's supervisors were also concerned and frustrated with Bob's inclinations. Although the school's policy permitted steady dating relationships among the students, the girls' supervisors agreed with Mr. Rice that it might help to talk with Trisha's dad.

Mr. Rice met with Arnold Slocum, Trisha's father. "Arnold, I think you know that Bob is dating Trisha. That boy doesn't have a very good track record, and we don't want to see Trisha get into trouble."

"Oh, yeah, that" responded Arnold. "Well, I don't like it very well, but what can you do when kids like each other? Pray a lot, I guess."

"But I think we might be able to help. If you don't want your daughter dating Bob while she's at school, we can enforce *that*. Just give the word and we'll see that she and Bob break it off."

"Thanks, George. I appreciate it. I'll talk it over with Virginia and get back to you. Okay?"

"I think it would be a good idea to do something soon. Bob and Trisha are getting pretty thick."

Arnold Slocum was a dynamic missionary with an impressive ministry in a rugged Andean village. He spoke with authority and confidence, but when it came to his children, it was Virginia Slocum, his wife, who called the shots.

Some time later, George asked Arnold what he had decided. "Well, Virginia and I talked it over and she thinks it's not going to be a problem. We know Bob and his parents pretty well. Virginia's sure we can trust the kids."

George later learned that Bob had been invited to spend three weeks in Trisha's home during the Christmas break. Only God, Trisha, and Bob know what liberties they had with each other during that time.

The following semester the leaders of the school met with Bob's parents to discuss the young man's dismissal for violations with another girl.

This was not an isolated story. I've known several passive Christian fathers in full-time ministry that were unable, too busy, or unwilling to protect their daughters. Some of these daughters may have retained their virginity, but we know that some of the girls lost theirs while they were on the mission field with their parents.

Shirley and I realized from such incidents that we had to be prudently vigilant in protecting our daughters from young men with *machismo* inclinations. Some of these fellows were good looking, polite, and friendly, so we could have been tempted to trust them. Sometimes our colleagues saw these fellows from a different perspective because of their friendship with them and suggested that we might be too protective. It would have been easy to let our guard down, because peer pressure not only affects teenagers, it can affect parents, as well.

Your wife (or husband) may insist that you "lighten up" and "not be so suspicious." Let's remind ourselves that Satan deceived Eve, and her husband followed her lead. *Machismo* exists among the "saved" and "unsaved," and those who practice it are aligned with this cunning "angel of light."

For the record, the vast majority of missionaries that I knew did a great job in training their children. The percentage of those whose children got involved in immorality was less than 5 percent, but the percentages increased after the 1960s and 1970s. An informal survey of graduates from our school indicated that over 85% of the students went on to be productive and effective Christians. Less than seven percent had fallen away. This indicated that missionaries' children we know did significantly better spiritually and morally than the average Christian youth in America. Such was the case in spite of the fact that many missionaries' children spend seven months a year in a boarding school. I believe this reflects parental faithfulness, not boarding school success.

Righteous Judgment

Just because Christians are appalled at the behavior of others does not exempt us from falling into the same sins. Given the right circumstances we may also fall, if not overtly, then perhaps in our imagination.

"Therefore thou art inexcusable, O man, whosoever thou art that judgest. For wherein thou judgest another, thou condemnest thyself; for thou that judgest doest the same things. But we are sure that the judgment of God is according to truth against them which commit such things" (Romans 2:1-2).

Very few normal boys or men with adamic natures are exempt from the possibility of developing *machismo* of heart, but I suppose a eunuch might be free from that temptation. In addition, most normal girls and women are vulnerable to the deceptions of men who have fine-tuned this behavior.

Worthless Salt

I believe a Christian who acts like an animal is confusing to non-Christians because people in the world expect God's people to have dignity and honor. The world despises promiscuous Christians and comedians in the media ridicule them. It seems obvious that unbelievers have no love or sympathy for single Christian girls who lose their virginity because they hold Christians to a higher standard than they have for themselves. That is to be expected since we are God's elect, His royal priests, and His chosen people. We are to be salt and light in a dark and ugly world.

Jesus said to his disciples, *"You are the salt of the earth: but if the salt have lost his savour, wherewith shall it be salted? it is... good for nothing, but to be cast out, and to be trodden under foot of men"* (Matthew 5:13).

If a Christian is involved in this conduct, we are not to fellowship with him. *"But now I have written unto you not to keep company, if any man that is <u>called a brother</u> be a fornicator, or covetous, or an idolater, or a railer, or a drunkard, or an extortioner; with such an one no not to eat"* (1 Corinthians 5:11 emphasis added).

The *Macho* is a Thief

The word "defraud" in I Thessalonians 4:6 means, "to cheat." One who cheats is a thief who steals through deception. When a young man takes physical affection from a girl who is not his wife, he is stealing from her future husband. He is also giving away what belongs to his future wife.

The girl is doing the same—cheating her future husband and her boy friend's future wife. When unmarried couples give their bodies and affection to each other they are defrauding their spouses (See I Thessalonians 4:5-7). Only a man and his wife have the God-given right to intimate affection that excites their passions.

When the Bible says, *"God is the avenger of all such,"* you can be sure there will be serious consequences. Often divorce is one of many consequences that result from defrauding. Divorces generate ugly experiences where additional complications can branch out like a wild vine that rapidly grows out of control. Divorce is like Asian kudzu vines in Georgia that seemed so right at first, but the rapid growing plants became a plague that smothered life out of trees and native vegetation.

We have all seen that whether a person is a Christian or unbeliever, no one escapes the fallout caused by violating God's standard.

Freedom from *Machismo*

Blessed is the Christian man who finds the wife of his youth God's way! Blessed are the father and grandfather who do all they can to protect their daughters and granddaughters, and who train their sons and grandsons to be men of dignity and honor.

"I have written unto you, fathers, because ye have known him that is from the beginning. I have written unto you, young men, because ye are strong, and the word of God abideth in you, and ye have overcome the wicked one. Love not the world, neither the things that are in the world. If any man love the world, the love of the Father is not in him. For all that is in the world, the lust of the flesh, and the lust of the eyes, and the pride of life, is not of the Father, but is of the world. And the world passeth away, and the lust thereof: but he that doeth the will of God abideth forever" (I John 2: 14-17).

Chapter 16

HOLINESS VS UNCLEANNESS

For God has not called us unto uncleanness, but unto holiness
I Thessalonians 4:7

When I think of the word *unclean,* the law of the leper in Leviticus 13 comes to mind. A leper was to announce his uncleanness to the world so that no one would get close to the incurable, contagious disease he had. *Concupiscence* therefore results in spiritual uncleanness just as leprosy makes one physically unclean.

A Christian who is truly regenerated by the Holy Spirit would accept the call to moral purity and turn away from uncleanness. Sheep do not enjoy the mud hole that delights the pig. Sheep follow their master whereas pigs must be driven.

I Thessalonians 4:7 tells us that all Christians have been called unto holiness. If we wish to reflect the Lord Jesus Christ, we will be pure in our sexual life, as well as in our attitudes toward others. *"Follow peace with all men, and holiness, without which no man shall see the Lord"* (Hebrews 12:14). We Christians demonstrate our relationship to our heavenly Father when we seek to be at peace with everyone by being morally clean and honorable.

This chapter is not about salvation, which is an *unconditional* free gift purchased for us by our Lord Jesus Christ. This is about "working out" that salvation (Philippians 2:12-16) which is living exemplary lives.

Holiness, not Behaviorism

Psychology has done damage to the Church by promoting the philosophies of man rather than the principles of God (Cp. Colossians 2:8). It amazes me that Christian leaders turn to philosophy (psychological methods and theories) rather than God's Word to find solutions to emotional and spiritual problems caused by sinful conduct. Why rely on men's theories when God tells us plainly what our trouble is and how to correct it? I will admit there are people with something mechanically or chemically wrong in their brains, but I'm addressing spiritual uncleanness that covers over 90% of our emotional and spiritual problems. Brain disorders may require tune-ups and chemical balancing. However, pills and theories cannot solve spiritual and moral uncleanness. That is God's business, who gives grace to the humble.

Classroom Casework, Counseling, and Combat

In 1975, I was taking a required course called "Casework Counseling and Corrections," part of a Masters' program of California State University, Chico. I entered the program, in part, as a means of integrating myself back into American society following several years in Bolivia.

Most of the people taking the counseling course were professionals who were upgrading their resumes—police officers, deputies, casework counselors, teachers, and a variety of county and state employees. It seemed all of us were in the process of dealing with the uncleanness in society. However, most of my fellow students were completely ignorant of God's standards and methods. They were leaning heavily on psychological methods to help morally dysfunctional people. Unfortunately, all of us were among the afflicted, including our instructor.

The instructor had implied there were no absolutes, only acceptable and unacceptable behavior as determined by current society. People with unacceptable behavior needed professional attention. Our teacher was presenting theories for helping people get back on track, and she reviewed various philosophies and psychological techniques, some old and some new.

I was disturbed by the philosophy of behaviorism and the promotion of relativism, so I asked the teacher, "Lori, I've heard a lot about acceptable and unacceptable behavior, and it seems the concept is quite subjective. Doesn't that leave it up to society and culture to determine what is acceptable? Aren't there some things that are just plain right or wrong all the time? For instance, I certainly would consider it wrong if Josh here broke into my car and drove off with it. That has to be wrong all of the time! Stealing is wrong. Cheating is wrong. People have been killed for cheating at poker."

Lori responded, "That's an interesting thought, Bill. Let's discuss it."

"Another thing," I added, "I wouldn't want a handsome guy like Burt to take my wife out for a weekend of pleasure in a motel. That would tear me up. That has to be wrong!" I also suggested that murder is wrong.

Well, the discussion got underway, and we covered most of the Ten Commandments without making one direct reference to them. God was never mentioned, and no "Christianese" was used by anyone. But the atmosphere in the classroom became very tense.

Lori was getting uncomfortable with the tension. She finally said, "Do you remember that I said it would be a good idea to break off a counseling session if you get that stiff feeling in your neck? Well, I'm experiencing that stiffness in mine, so let's take a break." The discussion had lasted only fifteen minutes.

I was also tense. Could it have been spiritual warfare in that classroom as God's Law exposed the darkness of humanistic philosophy? The professionals in that class had demonstrated a great deal of tolerance toward each other's opinions and practices. I wondered if they would have shown the same tolerance if I openly quoted Scriptures.

There was a pastor from a large denomination taking that class. As the semester progressed and familiarity increased among the students, so increased crude expletives. This pastor joined in with the coarse language. He seemed to be fully accepted.

I wanted to be a light and salt to my fellow students (Matthew 5:14-16). I was not alone. A deputy sheriff and a parole officer were also Christians and they were a great encouragement to me whenever I spoke out on something or asked questions.

Many of my Christian friends have chosen to follow the philosophy of psychology to deal with their sin problems. Psychology has become a very popular major in Christian colleges and it seems to help people feel better, like a drug that relieves the symptoms but leaves the infection. *"Whoso boasteth himself of a false gift is like clouds and wind without rain"* (Proverbs 25:14, Cp. Jude 12).

Why train our youth to become professional counselors using the philosophies and traditions of man? Shouldn't they be trained to become proficient ministers of God's Word? What philosophy can compete with the whole counsel of God? What psychological method can lead a wayward Christian away from uncleanness and iniquity to a life of holiness?

God's method attacks the uncleanness, provides a cure, and leaves a scar as a reminder.

Holiness, not Perfection

God's methods cure spiritual infections, and sound doctrine provides an understanding of realistic holiness.

Jesus said in Matthew 5:48, *"Be ye therefore perfect, even as your Father which is in heaven is perfect."* The word "perfect" might be better translated "complete" in the sense of full maturity. A mature disciple of Christ is one who seeks to understand how to love his enemies, how to pray effectively, to control his emotions and his body, and how to live at peace even with those who are offensive. He'll recognize when to turn the other cheek and resist rendering evil for evil, choosing rather to pray for those who do him wrong.

Therefore, this is not a call to absolute spiritual perfection, which may seem implied by the word "holiness." We are to seek after godliness in our conduct because of who we are and Who we represent.

"Now then we are ambassadors for Christ, as though God did beseech you by us: we pray you in Christ's stead, be reconciled to God" (II Corinthians 5:20). Ambassadors must be above reproach when representing their King.

How does one live a life of holiness? Paul told us how. He said to Timothy, *"Flee also youthful lusts: but follow righteousness, faith, charity, peace, with them that call on the Lord out of a pure heart"* (II Timothy 2:22). Genesis 39:7-12 gives us an excellent example of youthful Joseph resisting temptation when his master's wife sought to seduce him. His faithfulness to God landed him in prison where he got additional training for a giant ministry—Prime Minister of Egypt.

It takes time to develop character qualities, and for most of us, it takes longer than it should. Nobody seems to like discipline, but that is what it takes to escape uncleanness and live a life of holiness.

"Quick-fix" Theology

As a young Christian man with all normal chemicals active in my healthy body, several preachers told me that I could have a powerful life of holiness *instantaneously.* They assured me that if I would humbly, and with all of my heart, commit my life to Christ, God himself, would sanctify me completely by the Holy Spirit. They convinced me that I needed what was called a "second work of grace" from God. They said this experience would give me consistent victory over the world, the flesh, and the devil. I would be supernaturally empowered by the Holy Spirit in witnessing for Christ. Some preachers said this experience was the baptism of the Holy Ghost and evidenced by speaking in tongues. Someone referred to evangelist Dwight L. Moody receiving this special anointing and that his experience was an example of this empowerment.

Like many of my contemporaries, I longed for an experience that would empower me to live a consistent godly life, so I sought the experience many times. However, I never received any obvious supernatural empowerment. I continued to do battle with my fleshly desires, the world's influences, and the devil's deceptions—I lost some battles, and won some. Consistent victories, however, would have to wait until God brought into my life sound doctrine (See Titus 1:9).

I was open to this teaching on the "fullness of the Spirit," but I wanted the real thing—a truly supernatural transformation and empowerment. As I gained more knowledge of God's Word, I realized that not everything preached from the "sacred desk" is sound doctrine. I was discovering that there were many sincere preachers and teachers of *un*sound doctrine.

In my studies at a Bible school, I became convinced from Scripture that salvation was God's *unconditional* gift that sanctifies me (Titus 3:5-6)—*God's* righteousness, not *my* righteousness. Then I learned that sanctification was also a maturing and character building process that began when I presented my body to God as a living sacrifice (Romans 12:1-2). However, I did not learn the full significance of the practical sanctification of I Thessalonians 4:1-7 until 1975.

Nevertheless, I concluded that the Spirit baptizes all Christians into Christ the moment we believe the Gospel of Grace. *"But you are not in the flesh, but in the Spirit, if so be that the Spirit of God dwell in you. Now if any man have not the Spirit of Christ, he is none of his"* (Romans 8:9).

When I came to believe in Christ, I was zealous to share my new faith with anyone willing to listen. Since I was just a spiritual baby, I did not know what the fruit of the Spirit was, but I knew quite well what the fruits of the flesh were. I no longer had a foul mouth or a desire to please the world, and I was almost fanatically loyal to my wonderful Savior.

Before my salvation, I may have been considered generally honest and loyal to my family—a "good kid." Perhaps my parental training played a part in establishing some common virtues that many non-Christians practice. I had rejected smoking and drinking because of parental training and fear of addiction. However, I committed many sins that are embarrassing to relate, so pardon me if I don't shake out my dirty laundry (See Romans 6:20-21).

I cherished the peace that came with my salvation experience, and I wanted fellowship with Christ so much that repentance was easy. The area of self-control was where I faced my greatest battles that often ended in defeat and repentance. Repentance almost became a way of life, not for salvation, but for fellowship with my Lord (I John 1:9).

The lack of self-control affected my relationship with the godly girls that came into my life. They were as ignorant as I was regarding God's standards. What I know now explains why there was so much confusion in those uncertain years of dating.

Victory over anger was elusive. I would have done anything to find God's solution to that problem. The sermons on holiness often motivated me to "go forward" to receive the "sanctifying power" that would solve the problem of anger. I remember telling a fellow employee I was sorry for being rude to him five different times in one day. He mockingly said, "Bill, you're one of the sorriest guys I know!"

I suppose I would have even sought to speak in tongues if that would have helped. However, I noticed the lives of those who practiced speaking in tongues were not much different from mine. There simply was no shortcut to spiritual maturity—no "quick-fix."

Over time, I understood why the Apostle Peter wrote the following: *"And beside this, giving all diligence, add to your faith virtue; and to virtue knowledge; and to knowledge temperance; and to temperance patience; and to patience godliness; and to godliness brotherly kindness; and to brotherly kindness charity. For if these things be in you, and abound, they make you that ye shall neither be barren nor unfruitful in the knowledge of our Lord Jesus Christ" (2 Peter 1:5-8).* (Compare this progression in Romans 5:3-5. and the progressive characteristics of the Beatitudes in Matthew 5:3-12).

I was encouraged to realize that practical sanctification was a process and not a "quick-fix." The new birth in Christ brought supernatural sanctification by the indwelling of the Holy Spirit, but daily holiness of life was a maturing process requiring discipline, and discipline produced greater freedom from uncleanness. The Holy Spirit even led me to understand a practical solution to anger.

Anger, a Gift of God

We all know that anger has destroyed many marriages. A Christian controlled by anger may do some rash things. He could even commit murder or fornication.

Despite what conventional wisdom would have us think, to experience the emotion of anger is not necessarily sinful. I came to see that this emotion is a gift from God. In his book, "Competent to Counsel," Jay Adams helped me realize that the emotion of anger was a blessing and not a curse.

> *"Be ye angry, and sin not: let not the sun go down upon your wrath: neither give place to the devil"* (Ephesians 4:26-27).

What a relief—a person can be angry without sinning! But it is a dangerous emotion if not dealt with quickly and objectively. Uncontrolled anger is sinful and dangerous. Brooding anger is sinful and leads to "giving place to the devil" which leaves one open to evil suggestions and imaginations.

God has given us the emotion of anger, I believe, so that we will respond against injustices in this world. Anger, then, can be a virtue that warns us when something is wrong. When that which angers us is logically evaluated, we can focus on the problem and solve it.

A person who rarely experiences anger has a serious problem. For example, the passive father who is rarely angered by the behavior of his children could be more damaging than a dictatorial father might be. "Charley, you're playing with matches again. Your mother told you not to light them in the house. Oh, dear. You've got the curtains on fire again. Mabel! Charles's set the curtains on fire again."

Too many fathers are passive when it comes to leading the family spiritually. Later he groans over the consequences of being a self-serving and irresponsible leader of his own flesh and blood. More on this later.

Nevertheless, we experience anger most frequently when we are offended, our pride is hurt, or when we are inconvenienced. We find these experiences difficult to evaluate objectively, but it must be done if we are to avoid sinning. Holy living includes using our gift of anger properly. Would you believe it is possible for a Christian to be angry and filled with the Spirit at the same time?

Consistently Spirit Filled

Eventually, I discovered I was actually walking more consistently in the Spirit. Walking in the Spirit is the same as being filled with the Spirit, because we are controlled either by the flesh or by the Spirit.

"This I say then, Walk in the Spirit, and ye shall not fulfill the lust of the flesh. For the flesh lusteth against the Spirit, and the Spirit against the flesh: and these are contrary the one to the other: so that ye cannot do the things that ye would. But if ye be led of the Spirit, ye are not under the law" (Galatians 5:16-17).

"Therefore, brethren, we are debtors, not to the flesh, to live after the flesh. For if you live after the flesh, you shall die: but if you through the Spirit do mortify the deeds of the body, you shall live. For as many as are led by the Spirit of God, they are the sons of God" (Romans 8:12-13).

Many have been conditioned to believe that a person who is filled with the Holy Spirit is a Christian with exceptional spiritual powers, and not an ordinary disciple like most of us. All Christians who are free from known sin in their lives are filled with the Holy Spirit. It has to be that way; otherwise, Paul would have been unrealistic to command us to be filled with the Spirit *"And be not drunk with wine, wherein is excess; <u>but be filled with the Spirit</u>; Speaking to yourselves in psalms and hymns and spiritual songs, singing and making melody in your heart to the Lord; Giving thanks always for all things unto God and the Father in the name of our Lord Jesus Christ; Submitting yourselves one to another in the fear of God"* (Ephesians 5:18-21 emphasis added).

Did you notice? All of these are evidenced in the Spirit-filled life:
- Speaking to ourselves in psalms, hymns, and spiritual songs
- Singing and making melody in our hearts to the Lord
- Giving thanks for all things to God in Jesus' name
- Submitting to one another

Repentance, Confession, and Forgiveness

A lady asked me, "But I sin every day and ask forgiveness, don't you?" Yes I do, and so does every Christian who is honest with himself. It may seem that Ephesians 5:18-21 tells us *what to do* to be Spirit-filled, when in reality it is saying *what a Spirit-filled person does*.

In order for an offending Christian to be filled with the Spirit he must first confess his offenses and ask forgiveness of those affected by his sins, including the Lord. (Consider I John 1:5-10 which implies God has already forgiven and cleansed us the moment we confess our sins. However, to seek reconciliation with a person we must "put the ball in his court" by asking him, "Will you please forgive me? His positive response will clear up the matter... usually.) Once reconciled, the Christian will return to a Spirit-filled life with all of its blessings. Spiritually healthy Christians will know when the peace of God is gone, and they will want it back at all costs even humbling themselves to get it (Compare I John 1:9-10 with James 4:6-10 and I Peter 5:5-6).

What I'm addressing here is repentance. Repentance is nothing more than changing our mind about what we believe is true. We may believe we are innocent of a crime, but the evidence piles up and convicts us of the act. Then we change our minds and reluctantly agree that we are guilty.

All true Christians have two conflicting natures warring against each other for control of the mind (Cp. Romans 12:2). One is our "natural man" that the Bible calls the "flesh" which we inherited from Adam. The other is called the "new man" who is of Christ (Consider Ephesians 4:20-24 and I Corinthians 15:44b-17). Both the natural man and the new man live in our bodies, but, before God, the natural man is spiritually dead and the new man is spiritually alive (Romans 6:6-11 and Galatians 2:20).

Here's what I believe is going on: We Christians have moment by moment decisions to make during our waking hours. Our two natures are vying for control of our minds and those decisions. The flesh is totally selfish, self-centered, self-conscious, self-protecting, and it will encourage us to choose whatever is self-serving. The Spirit is God-centered and is concerned for Christ's reputation that He entrusted to us.

Let us say a person has bad breath, and he prefers to talk close and face-to-face to me making it difficult to avoid the odious gasses emitting from his oral cavity. As Christ's ambassador, I don't want to offend him, so I may search my brain for viable options to survive this ordeal. On the other hand, my self-centered flesh is crying out in anguish demanding relief from this insensitive polluter of my sacred space. If contempt takes hold of my mind, that means I have already made the decision to "despise" this person. Sin has been conceived. On the other hand, if I resist the temptation to be contemptuous, I am free to show him compassion for Christ's sake.

But let's say that I blow it and follow the flesh. I lose the peace of God and the joy of my salvation, and the Holy Spirit convicts me of this DRA (dirty rotten attitude). There is only one way to return to the Spirit-filled life—humility. I must confess my attitude to God, and the sooner the better if I want to minimize collateral damage. If my foul-breath friend has noticed my attitude, I must confess my DRA toward him as well, and say, "Mortimer, please forgive me for my cruel remark."

I don't care if it's bad breath, a loud vacuum cleaner, inability to communicate respectfully, a foolish statement, seeing a lewd photograph, interruptions, burnt toast, or bills piling up; the offenses and failures can be innumerable. The important thing is to recognize when an offense comes to mind and make the right decision—and when we fail, simply name it and confess it (I John 1:9-10). Let's not lie and say we didn't do it when the Spirit convicts us, otherwise we'll be calling God a liar.

Take heart, these things happen in every believer's life throughout the day, but we have a Great High Priest who intercedes for us (Hebrews 4:14-16), and we have the Holy Spirit who prays for us with *"groanings that cannot be uttered"* (Romans 8:26-

28). So, why not confess our sins and faults when we're guilty, *"and let the peace of God rule in [our] hearts, to the which also [we] are called in one body; and be...thankful"* (Colossians 3:15). It's all part of the maturing process and enables us to make eternal investments in heaven on a daily basis when we "keep short accounts."

I find it interesting that being Spirit-filled is compared to being drunk with wine. I recently had breakfast with a Christian who is addicted to alcohol, and he told me he understands that verse perfectly. For him, his life was either controlled by the Spirit or by booze. When his mind was saturated with alcohol, all kinds of uncleanness entered his life. When the Spirit controlled him, he was a blessing to everyone.

In Bible school I learned that the heart is deceitful and desperately wicked, which includes the hearts of Christians when they walk in the flesh. I used to believe that my Christian heart was not deceitful, but my personal record and the Scriptures proved that a false assumption.

"This I say then, Walk in the Spirit, and you shall not fulfill the lust of the flesh. For the flesh lusts against the Spirit, and the Spirit against the flesh: and these are contrary the one to the other: so that you cannot do the things that you would. But if you be led of the Spirit, you are not under the law" (Galatians 5:16-18). The Spirit-filled life is in reality the normal Christian life, a life that is charitably kind to others instead of self-serving and self-gratifying.

From Philadelphia to Laodicea

The local Bible believing churches and Bible schools used to be very concerned about the Spirit controlled life, as well as reaching the world for Christ. Thousands of disciples were sent all over the world with the Gospel. High moral standards were required of the missionary candidates who would be representing their Savior and their home churches. Schools like Multnomah School of the Bible, Moody Bible Institute, The Bible Institute of

Los Angeles, New Tribes Bible Institute, and Prairie Bible Institute were focused on preparing young men and women for careers in foreign and domestic missions.

Now the emphasis of many Christian fellowships has shifted away from holiness of life and careers in missions to "celebration," active worship, short-term missions trips, and "outreach." It is common to hear, "We must reach our community for Christ. Let's unite; put aside our doctrinal differences, and show this town true Christian love!"

Has the Church given up the emphasis of personal holiness in the lives of its people and decided to give them what they want? I recently read that one of the most popular evangelical preachers in America actually surveyed what his people wanted and organized his program accordingly. Could this people-pleasing approach be Laodiceanism? Consider Revelation 3:14-22.

A Bit of Greek and Roman Theology

When churches seek to please people they are open to the problem Aaron had with the Israelites while his brother Moses was receiving the Law on Mt. Sinai. Aaron was a people pleaser, so he gave them what they wanted—a golden calf idol, which they worshipped, and then they celebrated with a wild sex party. Israel paid dearly for this "uncleanness" when God had the Levites slaughter 3,000 men who refused to repent (not counting the women and children that may have perished). Idolatry and sexual uncleanness go together.

How did uncleanness and idolatry slither into our local churches? Slowly. It came in the form of a Roman god—Cupid, that erotic little god. *Eros* is his Greek name from which we get our word erotic—sexual love.

Romance became popular because of The Renaissance—the revival of Greek and Roman culture that had many gods, like Cupid. Note the *Roman* in *roman*ce. Fictitious romantic stories not fit to be revived, of heroes, heroines, and their loves were made for the attentive reading of an increasingly literate Western populace.

As more people read these tales, entertainment style romance largely displaced the parents' role in the courtship of youthful adults who had "fallen in love."

Ignorance of sound doctrine began to increase after World War I as many local churches relied on pulpit rhetoric instead of teaching "the whole counsel of God" (Cp. Acts 20:27). Progressively throughout the 20th century many Christians sought signs and wonders rather than God's wisdom, knowledge, and understanding. Many relied on emotional experiences, dreams and imagined revelations rather than on faith in God's Word.

Reviewing this sketch of history helps us know why many Christians are involved in some form of extra-marital uncleanness. It is tied in with idolatry.

Today, modern romance, as portrayed by the entertainment industry, is closely associated with *eros* (eroticism). Romance may be one of the pleasures of marriage, but romantic love or eroticism alone cannot keep a marriage strong and healthy. However, many people say their marriage is dead when romance is gone. That happens because their marriage was not established by vows before God and man, but upon fickle emotions.

Being ignorant of Scripture leaves pre-marital and post-marital couples vulnerable to their emotions and imaginations. It also affects their social conduct. The "going steady" and "breaking up" syndrome encourages many Christian young men and women to have a roving eye—ever looking for "true love." Sadly, this practice conditions them to be candidates for divorce and remarriage.

It is *agapao* (charitable behavior), and *phileo* (to love as a friend) that sustains the marriage. When *agapao* is practiced it produces *agape* (a charitable, compassionate attitude) in a man's heart for his bride.

Conclusion

Modern dating practices generally involve some level of spiritual uncleanness. Intimate sensuality outside of marriage is unclean, and those who engage in it are possibly preparing themselves for unnecessary frustrations, broken hearts, and possibly divorce. God would spare us from all of this. He has called us to holiness so that the world may see our good works and glorify our Heavenly Father. Holiness is not perfection, but a process of maturing and character building that all committed disciples experience. Our faithfulness may be rewarded with the expectation of a loving marriage that endures and blesses our children.

Chapter 17

HE WHO IS WISE

My son, be wise, and make my heart glad,
that I may answer him that reproacheth me
Proverbs 27:11

O Fear the LORD, ye his saints:
for there is no want to them that fear him
Psalm 34:9

A fourteen-year-old girl came up to Shirley and me following a presentation on "Dating, Courtship and Marriage God's Way" at a Christian school. She was not attending the school, but she joined the seminar because her parents, who were home schooling her, wanted her to have this opportunity. She said, "Bill, I'm so glad you gave this teaching. My parents have been instructing me in these things for a long time. It was encouraging to hear someone else outside of my family say these things. Thank you." So many families believe they are alone in their battles with evil and immoral forces in our culture.

Those who are supportive tend to be more reserved, whereas those who despise the teaching of I Thessalonians 4:1-8 are sometimes quite assertive.

Anyone may legitimately question the instructor's interpretations and applications of the Scriptures. That is good, because no man can say he has the last word on correct interpretation. People who carefully evaluate Bible teaching are "good Bereans" like those who searched the Scriptures when the Apostle Paul presented the Gospel at Berea (Acts 17:10-11). The "Bereans" do not bother me, but the person who hears the truth and rejects it is unwise.

"Wherefore be ye not unwise, but understanding what the will of the Lord is" (Ephesians 5:17).

Most people have limited knowledge of the Scriptures, so they simply accept what is taught. This places the responsibility on the teacher to be as accurate as possible and to avoid unbiblical agendas.

There are many in our nation and around the world that are seeking and finding God's wisdom. *"Ask, and it shall be given you; seek, and ye shall find; knock, and it shall be opened unto you. For every one that asketh receiveth; and he that seeketh findeth; and to him that knocketh it shall be opened"* (Matthew 7:7).

Singapore University Students

It surprised us to discover that people of other nations were often more receptive than American audiences. In 1994, twelve university students from Singapore accompanied my wife and me on a missions trip to the Philippines. Following a teaching session on "Dating, Courtship and Marriage God's Way" several students told us that they had never heard this teaching before. As I write this, there are three of those former students who are engaged and bringing their fiancés to us for pre-marital counseling.

Many students, young adults, and parents of various backgrounds have expressed gratitude for the verse-by-verse teaching from I Thessalonians 4:1-8. However, what would be the response from Christians who have experienced serious problems in their lives?

The Divorced

You might expect those who had suffered the trauma of divorce to be uncomfortable with this teaching. We have been pleasantly surprised. Some divorced Christians may have found the teaching "heavy," but there are those who have said they were grateful for the clear teaching on this subject. They only wished they had heard it before their first marriage. Clearly, the majority of godly Christians, no matter what their history, find straight teaching from God's Word on practical holiness edifying. It is too late to escape the consequences of bad decisions of the past, but they are motivated to escape future deceptions of the enemy.

Wise like a Pheasant

The pheasant has a short flight range, so it reserves flying as its last resort. More commonly, the pheasant uses camouflage as a defense, hiding itself from the predator, then running if necessary before the predator gets too close.

My father attempted to train me in the pheasant's art of self-defense when I was fourteen years of age. I was about to begin my freshman year of high school. That summer Dad and I were burning a small pile of trash on the dirt drive in front of our detached one car garage. We were leaning on our rakes, kicking sticks into the fire. Dad became very serious. He is a man of few words when it comes to serious talk, and God endowed him with a resonant bass voice that augments his authority. He wanted to teach me how to escape immoral girls.

"Bill! There's… uh… girls. Uh, *some* girls in…in that high school. They're no good, Bill. They can… Uh, they have…uhm… They've got bad diseases!" Some other words came out gruffly and haltingly. I have no doubt Dad's love motivated this brief admonition. It was very hard for him to speak about delicate social matters, but I understood fully what he was attempting to communicate. *There were immoral girls in high school that could destroy my life.*

It was not until my senior year that Dad's warning paid dividends. I found myself in a situation where I knew I could lose my virginity—that scene in front of the garage and Dad's words came back to remind me that I was in danger. I drove the girl to her home and dropped her off at the gate.

As I write this, I want to ask, "Why didn't our local church instruct parents on how to protect their children?" Not until seventeen years later did I hear candid instruction that I needed when I was twelve or thirteen (even earlier than that).

How my wife and I thank God for Dad's warning! He was faithful with the light that he had. I realize now that my parents' home, the local church, and the youth ministries had provided some protective "ground cover" even though it was sparser than it should have been. Many of my peers, both young men and women, fell prey to predators or became predators themselves.

A Troubling Trend among Women

In the '60s and '70s young women began smoking pot, taking hard drugs, giving their bodies freely to a variety of men, and becoming the aggressors in sexual relationships. As this trend increased in momentum, there became a noticeable shift in the Church. It became acceptable to "come as you are" to many evangelical churches that claimed to "be on the cutting edge" in reaching out to our culture. Not surprisingly, with a permissive attitude prevailing among popular "seeker friendly" church leaders a loss of personal dignity developed among young women.

Another inclination was running parallel to this development. Radical feminism eventually affected the evangelical Church, so much so that I Timothy 2:9-15; I Corinthians 11:3-10; and I Corinthians 14:34-36 were avoided by many Bible teachers. I've heard, "It stirs up people unnecessarily, and besides, it was written for a different culture and era. Women are more educated than they were in Paul's day." Therefore, I could not resist the temptation to address this subject indirectly with a group of high school and college students.

Shirley and I led a team of 24 students to Ivory Coast to do a missionary work project. Because of West African culture, all female members were required to wear dresses, and this cultural restriction was not popular with our young American women. I conducted Bible studies each morning and evening, but I wanted to have a third one during the lunch break. It would not have been prudent to announce my intentions, so I simply asked a provocative question at lunch time.

With a smile I asked our team members who were seated around our long, narrow table, "Who is it that determines proper clothing for ladies?" Several college girls turned their heads toward me and glowered.

"You're against pants, right!" one exclaimed with feeling.

"Could you just please answer my question. I just said, 'Who is it that determines proper clothing for ladies?'" I definitely had everyone's attention.

"You want us all to wear dresses, don't you!" another said with squinted eyes.

Again, still smiling, I restated my question, then appealed, "Please, just answer the question. It's 'who.' WHO determines what ladies wear?"

Their attack went on for about ten minutes, and the hostility increased so much that even some of the fellows joined the girls in challenging me. That surprised me more than the young women's reactions. However, in spite of the hubbub, I remained pleasant and calm. I knew I was "hitting pay dirt" with this question. I was very curious as to why this question generated so much hostility.

In the end, the girls admitted that women determine appropriate attire for girls and women, and that made sense to me and verified my suspicion.

I asked another question. "Aren't you ladies hoping to get married one day?"

Almost in unison came the answers, "Sure! Of course! We hope so." The hostility evaporated, and the girls now seemed curious as to where I was headed. Apparently, I was not such a bad guy after all.

"It seems to me," I said, "if you hope to get married sometime, you'd want to know what the men thought about what you wear."

"No way! You gotta be kidd'n! Men don't know what women want!"

"I find that strange. Perhaps the biggest event in your lives is getting married. Why wouldn't you want to dress to please your boyfriend or to get his input?"

"Why should we care what they think? They don't know about women's clothes, and besides, look at the way they dress."

"What about your parents. Doesn't your dad approve of what your mom wears?"

"Our dads couldn't care less. They hate shopping. That's a woman's thing."

"Well, that's not the way it is in our home. I'm not much of a shopper, but I am very concerned what my wife looks like when she goes out. She doesn't buy anything without my approval, and I value her advice regarding my clothing, too. The way we dress affects our public image. We are ambassadors for Christ, and we want to be sure we're good testimonies."

The lunch hour was nearly over, so I gave them my text for the Bible study we just had. It was Romans 12:1-2.

Later, Ruby, the only African-American person on our team, asked to speak with me privately. She was dressed in a disheveled manner—an oversized faded dress with a formless hat that gave her the appearance of a "bag-lady." She said, "Bill, you hit a sensitive note with me. I believe I've encouraged my half-sister to rebel against our dad. We didn't like his advice regarding our clothes, and about a lot of other things." She went on to explain that her mother dressed immaculately and normally sought her dad's advice and approval. Her mother was a radiant professional lady, but subject to her husband in almost everything. Ruby said she was going to ask her dad's forgiveness and help her sister become reconciled to him.

About five years later, Shirley and I were in Florida where Ruby and her husband were serving the Lord as Navigator missionaries. They invited us to dinner one evening. What a transformation! Ruby's hair and attire were immaculate and in excellent taste, as were her husband's. We felt like we were dining with celebrities.

Dad, my hope is that you will help fathers reclaim our right to be the heads of our homes so we can protect our daughters and wives from the destructive effects of radical feminism.

Protecting Your Own Body

> *Flee fornication. Every sin that a man doeth is without the body; but he that committeth fornication sinneth against his own body. What? know ye not that your body is <u>the temple of the Holy Ghost</u> which is in you, which ye have of God, and ye are not your own? For ye are bought with a price: therefore glorify God in your body, and in your spirit, which are God's* (1 Corinthians 6:18-20 emphasis added).

How is fornication a sin against our bodies? First, it is clear that each one of our bodies is the temple of the Holy Spirit. We are no longer separated from God like the unbelievers. What we do with our bodies includes the Holy Spirit. For that reason, there will be consequences for sinning against the temple in which He dwells.

The following are a few actual and potential consequences of the sin against the temple of the Holy Spirit ... our physical bodies:

- Becoming "one flesh" with an immoral person—*"What? Know ye not that he which is joined to an harlot is one body? for two, saith he, shall be one flesh"* (1 Corinthians 6:16)
- Children may be born and bear an undesirable stigma (Cp. Proverbs 5:15-17)
- Loss of the profound intimate love and pleasure God designed for husbands and wives (Consider Proverbs 5:19)
- Development of a reprobate mind that is unable to discern good from evil (See Romans 1:18-32)

- A loss of spiritual discernment (Hebrews 5:14)
- Forfeiture of spiritual leadership (I Timothy 3 and Titus 1)
- Creating an appetite for illicit sexual experiences (Romans 1:26-27; Cp. Colossians 3:5-6)

Stealing, blaspheming, covetousness, idolatry, rebellion, lying, and even murder are all outside of your body. Fornication, however, directly affects a person's physical body, and the human body will bear the consequences of fornication the rest of that person's life. Nevertheless, Christ paid for that sin just as He paid for all other sins (remember I John 1:9).

Sins before Salvation

Most people do not seek God's wisdom before salvation, so they commit sins that many Christians have escaped. What consequences are carried over into our new lives in Christ?

First, let us praise God that Christ died for all sinners, and no matter what our background, we can rejoice in our salvation.

> *"Therefore if any man be in Christ, he is a new creature: old things are passed away; behold, all things are become new"* (II Corinthians 5:17).

> *"I am crucified with Christ: nevertheless I live; yet not I, but Christ lives in me: and the life which I now live in the flesh I live by the faith of the Son of God, who loved me, and gave himself for me"* (Galatians 2:20).

A person who has lived a life of drunkenness, or been a thief, or even a murderer may find that grace has set him free to live a life he would never have dreamed possible. He might marry a Christian wife and raise godly children! A new life in Christ can result in great things indeed.

However, no sensible Christian would believe that the sins committed before salvation will not affect one's life even after regeneration.

> *"Be not deceived; God is not mocked: for whatsoever a man sows, that shall he also reap. For he that sows to his flesh shall of the flesh reap corruption; but he that sows to the Spirit shall of the Spirit reap life everlasting"* (Galatians 6:7-8).

If a person committed murder as an unbeliever, that person will still pay the penalty in this life for that sin even after salvation. Does that mean God has not accepted him and made him a son of God? Of course not. But the "baggage" that a murderer carries will be with him the rest of his natural life.

That principle also holds true for a man who was a fornicator prior to salvation. Through his faith in Christ, God fully accepts this man as wholly sanctified; but the act of fornication committed before salvation will affect his life after salvation. Although a fornicator can never recover his natural virginity, that does not affect a believer's new standing with God at all! Before God, that person is 100 percent holy because, in God's eyes, all of us who trust in Christ are "clothed" in "His righteousness" (Romans 3:24-26). God forgives and restores those who have committed homosexual acts as well. The blood of Jesus cleanses all who acknowledge and forsake their sins.

Nevertheless, the experience of fornication (including homosexuality) remains in our memories and must be a consideration when choosing a mate, especially if the potential spouse has been chaste.

NOTES

PART III

If we men practice personal holiness as discussed in PART II, we might be able to accept God's design for *domestic government*. It will take faith and courage, however. Our culture does not properly value authority and power in government, especially the most important civil government—the home. If you choose God's design, you will get no help from society, and you might get opposition from close friends and relatives. This is not a popular subject.

This section, therefore, is not written for cowards, but may be the most important part of the book. If you can appreciate godly authority in the home, this book will be a blessing.

For an appetizer, consider the following:

> Romans 13:1-2 *says, "Let every soul be subject unto the higher powers. For there is no power but of God: the powers that be are ordained of God. Whosoever therefore resisteth the power, resisteth the ordinance of God: and they that resist shall receive to themselves damnation* (condemnation or punishment)."

The word "damnation" in the King James Version is very strong by today's standards, but there is a reason for it. All governments have power and authority, and those who resist government will pay dearly for rebelling and in some cases, they will be executed. Most Christians do not realize how strongly God feels about authority, so I will quote what He said through Moses to Israel:

> *"If a man have a stubborn and rebellious son, which will not obey the voice of his father, or the voice of his mother, and that, when they have chastened him, will not hearken unto them: Then shall his father and his mother lay hold on him, and bring him out unto the elders of his city, and*

unto the gate of his place; And they shall say unto the elders of his city, This our son is stubborn and rebellious, he will not obey our voice; he is a glutton, and a drunkard. And all the men of his city shall stone him with stones, that he die: so shalt thou put evil away from among you; and all Israel shall hear, and fear" (Deuteronomy 21:18-21).

God did not seem to encourage reformation or rehabilitation programs when He established a system of law and order for Israel. You are probably glad that His system is not in place in the United States.

There is a chain of command in every government, and government in the home is no exception. Even democracies have a chain of command even though democracy is not God's ideal. Democracy is more Greek and Roman in principle than biblical. God has established a patriarchal system for The Church (elders), The Home (Dad), and His Kingdom (The King of Kings).

Stay with me and see if you don't find some of the thoughts in this section encouraging.

OUTLINE FOR PART III

Chapter 20
MOTHERS AND THEIR CHILDREN

CHAPTER 18

DAD'S AUTHORITY AND MOM'S POWER

Husbands, dwell with them according to knowledge, giving honour unto the wife, as unto the weaker vessel, and as being heirs together of the grace of life; that your prayers be not hindered
I Peter 3:7

Domestic Politics

God established the husband's authority in I Corinthians 11:3; what an eye-opener! When I understood this principle, I realized that whether Shirley submitted to my authority or not, I would still have my authority. I may not be a leader, or articulate, or good-looking, or "cool" like Clint Eastwood. I may be a wimp. She could even decide not to follow my leadership. Nonetheless, I am still the head of my home. There's no need to fight for that position because it's mine by divine right.

There's a catch, however. I have discovered I don't have as much *domestic political power* as Shirley does.

Let me illustrate with a story that did *not* happen. (We don't tell unpleasant true stories about ourselves. Our past offenses are forgiven, and we have agreed not to bring them up again. The following story, therefore, is fiction.)

I came home after my Friday PE class with the great idea of having a family picnic down by the riverside. Bolivia's *El Rio*

Pulquina at Tambo School is not a river but a creek, except when it floods. It has nice swimming holes and beaches and is a great place to have a picnic and "bond" with the family. At the supper table I announced to the family, "Hey, I've decided to take us all to the river for a picnic tomorrow! Isn't that a great idea?"

Well, I wasn't prepared for the response. No one seemed the least bit happy about my great idea. I looked at Shirley. She looked at me with her eyebrow raised. I looked at our four children who were looking at their mother. When they turned toward me, I saw four more raised eyebrows. With only a raised eyebrow Shirley had all of the kids lined up behind her. (I call that the power of the raised eyebrow). Mother and children had not spoken a word, but words were not necessary. It was disturbing. My manhood was threatened.

"What's goin' on here?" I demanded. "I get all fired up about a picnic and you guys are not with it? What's up, anyway?"

After our oldest children reached puberty, I had quickly learned that it was not wise to get into a delicate discussion with my wife in front of the kids. They had let me know that I looked like a 1000 pound Indonesian dragon whenever I defended my position. They always felt sorry for their mother, and rarely did they feel sorry for me. According to our custom, then, Shirley and I went to the bedroom for enlightenment.

"What's going on? I wanted to do something nice for the family, and you and the kids are against it.""Honey, don't get so worked up about it. We're not against you or your idea. I didn't want to tell you out there because it was a secret. We'd planned a surprise birthday party for you. Your birthday's tomorrow, remember? We've invited a lot of people."

"Oh."

Does this illustrate a typical situation in most homes? I believe Mom carries a lot of weight with the children. Dad gets upset because her influence over the children seems greater, especially when his plans meet resistance from Mom, and the kids follow her. If he gets angry, it only complicates his problem and strengthens the mother's position.

Dad is Responsible

We dads are responsible for the behavior of our children, their spiritual development, and their education. If they are not properly trained, it is primarily the failure of our administration (Consider I Timothy 3:3-5). A turning point for me came when I discovered I did not have the political power to fulfill this responsibility without the cooperation of my wife.

Shirley and I began early to prepare our children for godly courtship. Shirley's cooperation was essential. If she was not supportive, I had to discover why and reconsider my position. I had to learn that I couldn't demand respect or submission—those endowments were in Shirley's power to give or withhold. As our two oldest children started entering their adolescence, I came to appreciate Shirley's valuable counsel and began to view her power as an asset instead of a liability. With Shirley's support, it was much easier to lead our children.

Shirley has the power to strengthen or destroy our home (and so do I). I think Solomon had this in mind when he wrote, *"Every wise woman builds her house: but the foolish plucks it down with her hands"* (Proverbs 14:1). Fortunately, Shirley is a wise woman, and she has constructed a godly home.

Many women have tried to alter God's decree, but a wife cannot have equal authority with her husband. A woman with insight told me, "Bill, there are many wives who are not happy with "equal," they'll usurp the husband's rule. He'll let her do so, and a divorce is in the making." I agree that serious consequences befall a woman who resists this fundamental law of God. *"Unto the woman [God] said, I will greatly multiply your sorrow and your conception; in sorrow you shall bring forth children; and your desire shall be to your husband, and he shall rule over you"* (Genesis 3:16). Not only is it declared in the first book of the Bible that a husband would

rule over his wife, but it also works out best that way. Consider the following story as just one example of Shirley's need for my authority in the home.

We were on furlough and living in Redding, California when our daughter Becky was entering puberty. I came home one evening after painting signs to discover that Shirley was depressed.

People are often depressed because someone made them angry or offended them, and they chew on that offense until time or a remedy heals the pain. Hoping to help, I asked Shirley, "Did I do something to upset you?"

"No, that's not it."

"Well, what caused it?" I asked.

"Oh, I don't know. It just comes over me,"—her usual response to my usual question.

"Did the neighbor upset you?"

"No, we're fine."

"How about their dog?"

"No." (Dogs or cats don't usually make people depressed, people do).

"One of the kids?"

"Oh, yeah, that reminds me. Becky was demanding another glass of milk this morning, and she was nearly late for school. I told her to forget it and hurry out the door or she'd miss the bus. She was disrespectful and talked back to me. In her hurry, she spilled the milk on the floor. She made me so angry!"

"Did you deal with her attitude?"

"No, she was late, and I let her go."

"Well, when she comes home, I suggest you take her to the bedroom and have a little chat. If you need help, just let me know."

When Becky got home, Shirley took her to our bedroom and reviewed the conflict they had had that morning. Shirley applied practical psychology to the seat of the problem, gave some brief counsel, and then sought repentance and reconciliation. Both came out of the bedroom in fellowship, and Shirley's depression was gone. Several times over the years I had to back up Shirley's authority, which paid big dividends when I needed her backing.

Gifted Women

Shirley is not of less value, less gifted, or inferior to me, just different. In fact, she is a natural leader, a reluctant but effective public speaker, and a fantastic mother and counselor. It actually came as a surprise when it finally dawned on me just how gifted she was. After all, she was just a "damsel" when we married.

We fellows must face the truth. Some women are more intelligent, better leaders, and superior in knowledge than their husbands.

Nevertheless, our wives are subordinate by God's decree, not ours. Men have nothing to do with establishing domestic authority. (But some foolish men establish domestic tyranny in violation of Scripture).

Formerly, I would get angry, bluster, challenge, preach, and sometimes go outside and kick trees. It was so frustrating that my little 5'2" ninety-eight pound bride could challenge my authority and gain a following so easily! This situation was even worse when it happened with a group of young people with whom we had a ministry. It amazed me that Shirley, who had no political aspirations, was politically more influential in the home and the high school girls' dormitory than I who aspired to be a leader of my home and in ministry. Take, for instance, the following story:

One day I was returning from the basketball court where I had been directing a high school girls' PE class. Walking beside me was Rachel, a vivacious, gracious and respected student.

She said, "Mr. Pitt, there's something I think you need to know, but it is very difficult to tell you. Some of the girls are gossiping about you, and I think it is very unfair of them."

Oooh, she was so nice and gentle in the way she said that! And she let me know these treacherous girls were being unfair to my sacred person!

"They are saying that you are too harsh with your wife... It really bothers me to hear this, Mr. Pitt."

I thought, how comforting to know there was one sympathetic girl who stood by me, and she is spiritual besides. In reality, she was kindly preparing me for a whammy!

"Y'know, they're really wrong in gossiping about you, Mr. Pitt ... but, but, Mr. Pitt... uh... what they are saying is *true*." She was almost in tears of compassion as this tenderhearted girl smashed me right between my self-righteous eyes.

Well, Rachel gave me something to seriously consider. I knew my credibility was in jeopardy if the girls were disturbed by my conduct with my wife. I was politically in trouble with the very people I sought to influence toward godly living. So, the wise thing to do was to ask an experienced politician.

I asked Shirley, "Honey, am I too hard on you at times?"

"Why do you ask? I guess there are times when I think you are a bit harsh, but I suppose I deserve it." Now, isn't that just like a spiritually correct person.

"Well, Rachel said some of the girls are gossiping about me and saying I'm too hard on you. Rachel agrees with them, too. So, tell me. Am I too hard on you?"

"I think you are sometimes. Yes. But, then, you always try to get things right. I guess they aren't really being objective because I'm certainly not faultless." (I really am a blessed man to have such a prudent wife.)

I finally got the picture. The truth was, I was harsh, manipulative, and even unreasonable, but at first I did not like knowing the blazing truth.

What did I learn from all of this? I can hardly wait to tell you.

Executive Power

I have observed and experienced "The Power of the Executive Officer." Since I'm the captain of the Pitt Ship, Shirley is the executive officer, the second in command.

As I see it, there are three ways to captain a ship. You can be a tyrant who runs it with an iron hand. You can be an irresponsible coward, leave the decisions to the Exec, and then take credit for the things that go well. Or you can run it God's way. I suppose you'd like to know how to do it God's way.

Your own understanding probably won't help you. *For my thoughts are not your thoughts, neither are your ways my ways, says the LORD. For as the heavens are higher than the earth, so are my ways higher than your ways, and my thoughts than your thoughts"* (Isaiah 55:8-9). This means you will be in for a surprise. Jesus gave us the answer and so did the Apostle Paul.

Jesus told us that the greatest among His disciples would be the servant of all the rest (Cf. Luke 22:24-27). In fact, He, the God of all creation, said He came to serve, not to be served.

Paul told husbands they were to be willing to lay down their lives for their wives just as Christ laid down His life for the Church.

> *"Husbands, love your wives, even as Christ also loved the church, and gave himself for it. That he might sanctify and cleanse it with the washing of water by the word. That he might present it to himself a glorious church, not having spot, or wrinkle, or any such thing; but that she should be holy and without blemish. So ought men to love their wives as their own bodies. He that loves his wife loves himself"* (Ephesians 5:25-28).

Obviously, Christ, as God, is the greatest leader and authority of all. If He laid down His life for His Church (his Bride) and set the example of servant leadership, then you as a Christian man are not weak if you do the same for your bride. What's more, Christ made no demands on his Bride, the Church. However, whenever any one of the members of His Church offered themselves as living sacrifices, He gave them opportunities of service that were extremely rewarding. In like manner, a husband who gives his wife freedom might have the joy of receiving sacrificial service like Shirley gives me. The secret: make no demands on her, and reward her with praise for all she does for you voluntarily.

A strong man is one who serves his wife and gently asks for her point of view on most serious matters affecting the family. I'm not saying that you find out how she's thinking and then do it her way. What I'm suggesting is to listen to her and then do the right thing.

A Reminder

In this study, our objective is to help our children follow God's way in finding a wife or husband. In order to succeed in this, Mom and Dad must be together (Review Ephesians 5:22-33). A divided home is worse than weak *"...Every city or house divided against itself shall not stand"* (Matthew 12:25c). When I serve Shirley by showing her the respect she deserves and including her in important decisions, I don't have to worry about her superior domestic power with the kids.

A wise leader will know the importance of getting counsel from his subordinates, including the children. Don't tell me you are not a leader, Dad. All husbands are leaders, whether good leaders or bad leaders. Even incompetent or wimpy leaders can do well if they have a good executive officer to back them up and give counsel.

Executive officers are in a better position to assess the consequences of the leader's blind areas. The Exec may also have a better understanding of the mind of the subordinates because the Exec is one himself (herself). All leaders need counselors to protect their backs. The foolishness of the indecisive captain in the story "The Caine Mutiny" was not his lack of authority. It was his distrust and rejection of counsel from his executive officer and other subordinates. His pride and fears kept him bound by his weakness.

You've heard a lot about women's intuition. Could it be that the little lady has this attribute because she, a subordinate herself, knows where the kids are coming from? If she has this ability, wouldn't it be wise to seek her counsel? Of course! Blessed is the dad who taps Mom's wisdom.

The King's Power

King David succeeded in defeating his son Absalom's military bid for the throne of Israel because of a loyal, wise counselor. God had raised up Hushai to advise David in military and political matters. David also had a second counselor, Ahithophel, who joined Absalom's rebellion. David sent Hushai to counter the wisdom of Ahithophel. So successful was Hushai's undermining of Ahithophel that the latter knew he was defeated and committed suicide. Ahithophel was confident his counsel to

Absalom was superior and could have brought about a victory. When Ahithophel saw he was undermined, he knew David would win. Ahithophel also knew he would be executed for his betrayal. (You can read this fascinating story in II Samuel 15 through 17.)

Wives have the power of counselors like Hushai and Ahithophel. They may have the wisdom to save the home from disaster if the king of the castle will listen to the queen and her children. Her loyalty to the king, however, is a very important factor. Wise Hushai was loyal to his king. Wise Ahithophel was unfaithful to his king and tried to destroy him. Faithful Hushai had both prudent and godly wisdom. Traitor Ahithophel had only prudent wisdom. Blessed is the husband with a loyal wife who has prudent and godly wisdom, for she is priceless.

"Who can find a virtuous woman?
for her price is far above rubies.
The heart of her husband does safely trust in her,
so that he shall have no need of spoil.
She will do him good and not evil all the days of her life"
(Proverbs 31:10-12)

"House and riches are the inheritance of fathers:
and a prudent wife is from the LORD"
(Proverbs 19:14)

A wise, loyal wife with a heart like Hushai's will be vitally concerned about the affairs and success of her husband. That is especially true in matters affecting the children and their children's choice of a life partner. However, a clever, self-serving wife could become like Ahithophel and betray her husband in pursuit of her own interests. She could destroy her husband (and her family) if God does not intervene. *"A virtuous woman is a crown to her husband: but she that maketh ashamed is as rottenness in his bones"* (Proverbs 12:4).

A Three-strand Cord

Who, then, was the most powerful in David's kingdom—the king who sat on the throne, or he who gave the king counsel? Wisdom is always more powerful than authority, but authority with wisdom is like a two-strand cord.

"Through wisdom is an house builded;
and by understanding it is established:
And by knowledge shall the chambers be filled
with all precious and pleasant riches.
A wise man is strong;
yea, a man of knowledge increases strength.
For by wise counsel you shall make your war:
and in multitude of counselors there is safety"
(Proverbs 24:3-6).

 When Dad and Mom are together they have the authority and the power to control the kids. The children are more likely to accept their parents' admonitions regarding the challenges of life. If they do, that will make a very strong family. A three-strand cord is strong indeed!

Two are better than one;
because they have a good reward for their labour.
For if they fall, the one will lift up his fellow:
but woe to him that is alone when he falleth;
for he hath not another to help him up.
Again, if two lie together, then they have heat:
but how can one be warm alone?
And if one prevail against him,
two shall withstand him;
and a threefold cord is not quickly broken
(Ecclesiastes 4:9-12)

Family unity is essential if the children are going to stand against peer pressure and the philosophies of the world. Courtship and parental involvement are strange concepts to many in our modern culture. Yet your children will need united parents who can help them when their peers label them with names like "strange, weird, and fanatics."

A Foolish Wife?

What if a wife is not wise? That indeed is a problem—if she truly is unwise. Sometimes she may only appear to be unwise, or she may have been driven to unwise behavior because of the foolishness of her husband. Perhaps the following story will illustrate how men might underestimate their brides.

Shirley was not the least bit sophisticated, in fact she had lived her last four teenage years on a primitive cattle ranch. The ranch was on a large *pampa* (grassland) surrounded by a thorn forest known as the Green Hell of Paraguay, South America. By contrast, I had gone to three different colleges, spent two years in the army, and lived in Chico, California most of my life. Shirley was twenty years old and I was twenty-seven.

I had not taken into account the gifts, experience, education and abilities of my future wife. Her attractive features and sweet innocence were far more important to me at that time than sophistication. Among women, there were few jewels like my bride to be; however, her lack of sophistication and her guilelessness resulted in humorous verbal responses.

When Shirley and I were close to our wedding day, some newlywed friends invited us to take a ride through the Wisconsin countryside. I had been an art education student, and I often saw a setting that seemed like a good subject for a painting or a sketch. After viewing many picturesque farms and other potential country compositions, I spotted a nearly perfect candidate. "See that barn over there? I exclaimed, "I would like to paint that."

Shirley responded, "It sure needs it!"

Our friends and I laughed at this innocent response. I didn't realize it then, but my fiancée had just given me a glimpse of the practical intelligence God had given her—something designed to balance a visionary husband. *"House and riches are the inheritance of fathers: and a prudent wife is from the LORD"* (Proverbs 19:14).

Not only was Shirley a contrast to my temperament and educational background, she also saw things from a woman's point of view. (For example, she questions my use of the words *domestic political power*. She prefers the words *parental influence* better, and our daughters agree with her). She was more concerned about the price of groceries than the engine in our car. She saw the importance of listening to our children before I did. She feminized the decor of our house. Submission to leadership came easier for her, while I had to deal with a competitive spirit. Furthermore, when our oldest daughters were in their later teens, Shirley and the girls could be talking at the same time and still understand each other. That still goes on at our house whenever our daughters and their teenage daughters are visiting. The noise reminds me of a turkey farm. Now please don't say I've called my wife a turkey.

It is obvious that most women do not think like men. They do not normally go for crass or coarse speech. A few might enjoy talking about secretions, belching and body odors, but not my bride. She appreciates good manners. She and two of our three daughters are into flowers, frills, trinkets, and do-dads of all kinds. They like perfumes, skin cream, body wash, lace and doilies. One of the girls appreciates these things to a lesser degree, and prefers finding bargains at a thrift shop. God sure knew what He was doing when He created Eve to help Adam.

Prayer

In my job—teaching Bible to high school students—I couldn't afford to go a day without the Lord answering my prayers. Some of the most intense spiritual warfare takes place in high school classrooms. If I had a bad attitude toward Shirley, I knew I would be in trouble with the Lord. *"Husbands, live with [your wives] according to knowledge, giving honor unto the wife, as unto the weaker vessel, and as being heirs together of the grace of life; that your prayers be not hindered"* (I Peter 3:7).

It took years to adequately apply I Peter 3:7 to my life. I found that when the going got rough, I began to seek the education that Shirley had for me. I had to learn to listen to what she said and evaluate it objectively. If she was reluctant to tell me, I had to gently ask her questions. When I truly wanted to know how she really, I mean *really*, viewed something, I could generally find a way to get her to tell me. *"Counsel in the heart of man [or woman] is like deep water; but a man of understanding will draw it out"* (Proverbs 20:5).

The realization of our own complexity was a big help to Shirley and me. Husbands and wives may think they know each other, but we all have to remember that the Creator made us, and He made us in His own image—very complex. Therefore, we should not try to estimate the value of each other or impetuously judge the other's private motives. I get tempted a lot in this area.

The Apostle Paul wrote, *"It is a very small thing that I should be judged of you, or of man's judgment: yea, I judge not mine own self. For I know nothing by myself; yet am I not hereby justified: but he that judges me is the Lord"* (1 Corinthians 4:2b-4).

Jesus also warned against judging another person's motives in Matthew 7:1-2: *"Judge not, that you be not judged. For with what judgment you judge, you shall be judged: and with what measure you mete, it shall be measured to you again."*

Righteous judgment of evidence is encouraged, however, especially if you are an authority like us dads. *"Do you not know that the saints will judge the world? And if you are to judge the world, are you not competent to judge trivial cases? Do you not know that we will judge angels? How much more the things of this life!"* (I Corinthians 6:2-3).

Emotions

What if Mom is wrong and has a blind spot? What if she is being controlled by emotions? I've seen this happen several times with a variety of women. Emotions and blind spots affect us all, but the ladies, I believe, tend to be more emotional than men, generally speaking. (Feel free to disagree.)

Here's what I suggest. Keep your cool; be gentle and respectful, and state your case. Dad has the authority and the right to tell Mom she is wrong, and you should explain to your wife why she is wrong. If she is still convinced she is right and insists on doing it her way, you have a different problem. If you don't get her attention, you cannot help her. There are women who can't seem to control their emotions or their tongues (like some men). Once she is out of control, she may drive you crazy with cascading verbiage that overloads the best of brains. Consider the following story:

Dr. Arnold Busch was telling me about his wife Heather who had a frantic way of responding to life's frustrations. The gentle doc was himself one of her major frustrations because of his tendencies to respond slowly to domestic problems. He said he was quite willing to discuss any problem, but he couldn't get her to stop yelling, crying, and attacking him—sometimes physically!

A problem like this requires serious prayer. So I prayed for wisdom.

This was what came to mind. I said, "Arnold, you must first get her attention. I suggest you hold your hands up with your palms facing her and say, 'Hold it!' If she keeps talking say, 'Hold it' again. It may take a few of these firm commands. When you can, tell her you will handle the problem when she stops talking."

Arnold did just what I suggested and it worked. Of course, I told him to concentrate on the problem and not on her offenses. Once Heather was listening, Arnold was able to ask her to forgive him for his offenses, if indeed he was guilty of something. Heather was then free to help Arnold arrive at a solution to the problem.

Higher Authority

When our wives insist on going against our authority, there is little we can do to prevent it. What I suggest to say is, "Honey,

I see you are insisting on having your way even though it is not wise. I have no alternative but to let you do what you plan to do (provided it isn't murder). But I want you to know that what you are doing is wrong. So, I'm turning this matter over to the Lord. I'm going to pray right now that God will help us both."

This is not being weak—on the contrary, it is good leadership to acknowledge our limitations. A good motto is "Keep cool; God is near." We have a right to seek higher authority over the actions of a rebellious person who is under our authority. We have the Lord Jesus Christ. He is our higher authority, and His power is unlimited. *"I would have you know, that the head of every man is Christ; and the head of the woman is the man; and the head of Christ is God"* (I Corinthians 11:3).

Christ is honored when we acknowledge His Lordship when our position is challenged. There may be times when we have no other recourse but prayer. When we are powerless, Christ's strength is available. *"[Christ] said unto me, 'My grace is sufficient for you: for my strength is made perfect in weakness.' Most gladly therefore will I rather glory in my infirmities, that the power of Christ may rest upon me"* (II Corinthians 12:9).

He has promised that we will not have a test that is too much for us to bear, but with the temptation make a way of escape. *"There has no temptation taken you but such as is common to man. But God is faithful, who will not suffer you to be tempted above that you are able; but will with the temptation also make a way to escape, that you may be able to bear it"* (I Corinthians 10:13).

Some men resort to harsh commands and even violence. Such actions and reactions reveal emotional inability and a lack of wisdom. No matter how intelligent, worldly wise, or how successfully he may lead other men; any man who is reactionary and wrathful is not strong. This problem demands getting help from a trusted brother in Christ who knows God's Word, and has discernment—and the sooner the better. These men are available, but they will not come looking for candidates. *"Counsel in the heart of man is like deep water; but a man of understanding will draw it out"* (Proverbs 20:5). Therefore, if you have a problem with anger, you must take the initiative to find a solution.

I've experienced this lack of self-control to my shame. Kenneth Taylor's "The Living Bible" addresses this weakness more directly than the Authorized Version: *"The fool who provokes his family to anger and resentment will finally have nothing worthwhile left. He shall be the servant of a wiser man"* (Proverbs 11:29). This warning motivated me to study the Scriptures and read books on the subject. Jay Adams' books "Competent to Counsel" and "The Christian Counselor's Manual" were a great help.

We all appreciate the man who controls himself, carefully assesses a problem and looks for a biblical solution. Such a man prays for wisdom from God and seeks counsel from trusted friends. His closest friends are his wife and children.

Conclusion

Blessed are the children with a father and mother who are loyal to each other, respect each other's wisdom, and understand the difference between authority and power in domestic matters.

Chapter 19

DADS AND THEIR CHILDREN

"For I know [Abraham],
that he will command his children and his household after him,
and they shall keep the way of the LORD,
to do justice and judgment;
that the LORD may bring upon Abraham
that which he hath spoken of him"
Genesis 18:19

Where the Buck Stops

Both Abraham Lincoln and Harry Truman proved to be greater men than people realized at the time. Both came from humble backgrounds, had failed often in business and politics, and had married women that were more liability than asset. Neither one had great speaking voices. One was tall and lanky; the other was short and bespectacled. However, both had authority, took their responsibilities seriously, and did what they believed was the right thing. Truman said, "The buck stops here."

Dad, as the head of your home, the "buck" stops with you. If you accept your headship in a gracious manner, your wife and children will be blessed of God.

Who knows, you may, like Abraham, become the father of a great nation.

"For I know [Abraham], that he will command
his children and his household after him, and
they shall keep the way of the LORD, to do
justice and judgment; that the LORD may bring

upon Abraham that which he hath spoken of him"
(Gen 18:18 KJV).

The Consequences of Adam's Sin

Adam had also been in a position of leadership; in fact he was the leader of the entire world population (Eve and himself and all living things) before he sinned. Adam could have protected Eve from the deception of Satan, but he was either absent, passive, or simply curious. The reality was *both* received severe consequences, including death, but it was Adam, not Eve, who brought sin upon all succeeding generations (Romans 5:15), and his sin also affected all of creation (Romans 8:19-21). The principle we learn from this and many other stories in the Bible is that an irresponsible head of the family brings serious consequences on a home and beyond the home. Just consider what happened to King David's family and his nation after he sinned with Bathsheba.

It is frightening to realize what could happen to my family when I sin. The wages of sin are death even for Christians—not eternal death in hell, but death nevertheless (consider lost opportunities). What greater reasons have we to pray than this? No wonder Jesus urged us to pray *"And lead us not into temptation but deliver us from evil [the evil one], for thine is the kingdom, and the power, and the glory forever."* The evil one has targeted us.

Christ's great enemy, who is our enemy too, is doing all in his power to discredit us dads.

The entertainment industry, which I believe Satan influences, has been mocking us for a long time. It has stereotyped us as lacking common sense, foolish in decision-making, and thoughtless jerks that need constant correction by a sensible wife and "cool" kids. This is considered comedy in the world of entertainment, and in the commercials of those who sponsor these productions. There is no need for me to go into details because it is obvious that most commercially produced entertainment is designed to damage our spiritual strength.

Some productions that are called "family entertainment" attack our dignity, teach our children to speak disrespectfully to us and their mothers, justify lying, mock Christianity, and promote humanism.

No doubt, the principal targets for spiritual destruction are Christian fathers and Christian young men and boys. Certainly, the unbelievers are also adversely affected. However, faithful Christian fathers are a profound threat to the objectives of Satan. We invade his territory, and he doesn't like that at all. *And the dragon was wroth with the woman, and went to make war with the remnant of her seed, which keep the commandments of God, and have the testimony of Jesus Christ*" (Revelation 12:17). The "woman" is Israel, and the "remnant" is the universal assembly of Christ's disciples. Every Christian family suffers spiritual, physical, and emotional attacks from the dragon that influences this present world system. The husband/father is Satan's primary target.

We men are the main targets of God's enemy because we are the primary hope for rearing a godly family. This is biblically and sociologically true; if a choice had to be made before God as to who should rear your children, you, Dad, are the best qualified, *not* Mom.

A simple consideration of what is happening to single-mother homes will demonstrate the truth of that statement. A comparative study between single-mother homes and single-father homes would bear this out. (Don't even consider the homosexual or criminal issues when contemplating such a study).

God knows fathers are more essential to the development of godly children than are the mothers (See Genesis 18:19). Before this sociologically incorrect statement ruins your objectivity, please stay with me with an open mind (Romans 12:2). This discussion is not anti-mother, anti-woman, or "chauvinistic." It is a conviction based on logic and my understanding of the whole of Scripture. I will not overlook the tremendous influence of a faithful mother or grandmother.

A Mother's Handicap

My wife, Shirley, has an equally important role in our two-parent home. Nevertheless, she is lacking the God designed masculine authority by which I typify God's presence before His children. As a feminine subordinate, Shirley is naturally impeded if she is forced to take the role as head of the home.

These days it does not require a professional study to see the discouraging results of single-mother families. The media saturates us with stories that underscore my position here. President Lyndon Johnson's "War on Poverty" made it possible for unwed mothers and parasitical men to mass-produce children at government expense. These children often never know who their fathers are, and they grow up in a matriarchal society where sadness, grief, immorality, abuse, and crime are rampant. For our authority on this, watch the evening news.

California, the "Golden State," has become the easy no-fault divorce "Welfare State." Shameless politicians maintain their power by buying votes from welfare recipients, many of whom are unwed mothers. This practice reaps the same as Johnson's policies—fatherless homes with all of the fall-out. Los Angeles is the "drive-by-shooting" capital of the world.

Unwed mothers, generally speaking, do not have the ability to control their families. Without Dad's authority, the family ship lacks the authority to control the crew. We are speaking in general terms, of course there are exceptions.

Widows and the Fatherless

We must make a distinction between the unwed mother homes and homes of widows. The latter has Bible promises that assure the widow that God has special provisions for her as she walks in the Spirit. Here is one example of several: *"A father of the fatherless, and a judge of the widows, is God in his holy habitation."* (Psalm 68:5). There is no stigma attached to a godly widow. God is the father of her children.

Perhaps some of the promises apply to the divorced mother too, but in her case she has extra complications because the father of the children is usually still alive and is often viewed as an enemy.

However, there are serious complications in the lives of unwed mothers who continue to produce children. She and the men involved with her pay dearly for their actions, and sadly, so do their offspring.

Family Unity

Children are born with rebellion in their hearts (Cf. Psalm 51:5); therefore, it is natural for a child to follow a permissive parent more readily than the one who seeks to train him biblically. That is why family unity is very critical. A dating couple should seriously discuss their biblical world views before entering a courtship that might lead to marriage.

What happens when one parent is following biblical principles, and the other parent tends to be permissive or rebellious?

If Dad is the only parent who holds to biblical principles, the children would be more inclined to follow the Lord than if Mom alone is the faithful one. I am sure there are many exceptions to this general observation, but I believe my assertion is verifiable. Nevertheless, to have the best chance at success in training children to resist sinful inclinations, it will take the combined faithfulness of two godly parents.

A faithful spouse will find prayer a major source of power and comfort when reasoning seems to be ineffective in gaining unity with a rebellious spouse. God is very interested in the development of our children, but disunity between the parents will cloud God's counsel. Prayer is an appeal to God to act when your authority or power is limited by evil forces greater than you are. You, dad, will be wasting your time praying, however, if you are not in fellowship with your wife (I Peter 3:7).

Why am I addressing this subject of unity to you, Dad, when Mom may need the same reminder? It is because you are responsible to maintain unity. Later I will discuss how we dads can biblically maintain unity and peace in the home.

Philosophies and Traditions of Man

Philosophies and traditions of man have permeated most local churches. It is increasingly *unacceptable* to teach biblical child discipline and training in the local churches. Now we need expert knowledge from "qualified professionals" to instruct us in the complexities of rearing fragile "innocent" human beings. We are urged to seek expert advice to keep us from corrupting the innocent because we are tainted by the primitive upbringing of previous generations.

My wife and I often discovered veiled contempt for biblical teaching on child training while working among Christians in

Singapore. Philosophies of men, both Western and Eastern, were more popular.

There were many Christians in Singapore, however, who were hungry for the truth, and some of the young parents were desperate. Their children were out of control. What these believers had learned at school, church, from parents, and from their peers simply did not work.

One of those who preferred God's wisdom was a superior court judge. His children's controlled behavior was a contrast to those of other families in their church Cell Group (CG).

If Mom is into humanistic psychology, Dad, you have a serious problem. In fact your problems are similar to what Solomon faced when he married too many heathen concubines. They actually seduced the wisest man on earth into worshiping their gods. However, you have an advantage over Solomon. Your wife is sanctified because you belong to Christ. Solomon's wives were not sanctified in that way. In addition, you can appeal to God to work in your wife's heart and change her mind.

This may not work as effectively for the wife, but just the same, an unbelieving husband is also sanctified by being married to a believing wife (I Corinthians 7:14).

When I was a teacher and administrator in a Christian school, my colleagues and I often discussed appropriate discipline of high school students who committed serious infractions. We all favored consequences of some kind for students who showed no remorse for their behavior. However, there was always someone, it seemed, who insisted on giving grace and withholding consequences if a student appeared contrite.

We all wanted to be compassionate, so our practice was not to punish those students who repented, but to show "grace." (I put *grace* in quote marks because it wasn't true grace but appeasement.)

Some of my colleagues appeared to be exceptionally gifted in leading students to repentance, but there was a hitch. A few high school boys were talented penitents. They could actually control their tear ducts. When they were caught in a serious violation, these fellows became experts in contrition. On came the water works. With tears pooling between their feet, the culprits would pour out their confessions and promises to go straight. My colleagues were ultimately disillusioned when we caught our contrite students mocking our "inquisition" before their roommates.

From then on, my colleagues and I verbally forgave their offenses but physically applied psychological motivation. We endeavored to administer some form of punishment for each overt infraction the high school students committed. We would say, "Brad, I gladly forgive you for what you have done, but you must receive the consequences for what you did." We got a lot of work projects completed around the school.

If Brad had asked why he was punished after asking for forgiveness, we would explain why. Bible doctrines are often best taught in the midst of life's experiences. My colleagues needed to consider more carefully why God punishes His children, and allows those who are not His children to continue in their sins without immediate consequences (See Hebrews 12:5-13). What strong language we find in this chapter of Hebrews—*"If you be without chastisement, of which all are partakers, then are you bastards, and not sons."*

When we administrators withheld "chastisement" from our high school students we were not treating them as loving parents would. We were taking a convenient way to sidestep an unpleasant responsibility. As overseers of the souls of these young people, we were demonstrating a fear of man rather than God, and love of ourselves rather than God's children. We should have known why God was so severe with King David even though the king confessed his sins and demonstrated a contrite heart. (Read the story of David's great sin with Bathsheba and the consequences in II Samuel 11-15. Also consider the discipline he suffered in II Samuel 24.) God will not be mocked, and we had a responsibility to teach that lesson to our students. We were encouraging them to mock the standards of our school.

Dad and Mom cannot afford to be mocked either, because the price of appeasement is simply too high—it could destroy the child's potential and worse. Consider what the wisest man who ever lived (not counting Christ) said, *"Withhold not correction from the child: for if thou beatest him with the rod, he shall not die. Thou shalt beat him with the rod, and shalt deliver his soul from hell"* (Proverbs 23:13-14).

Children who are blessed receive the consequences for their actions quickly. Those who escape immediate consequences experience life-altering damage to their character, and they may end up in hell forever (Cf. Revelation 20:10-15). Prisons are full of men whose fathers were irresponsible. These men send Mothers' Day cards donated by a card company, but they send very few Fathers' Day cards.

Responsible dads are indeed the key to a strong United States of America.

Good Dads Lead in Child Training

There are only two basic principles to keep in mind when it comes to rearing children God's way:

- Train our children to obey and respect our authority
- Actively love our children by being faithful, gentle, firm, and consistent

> *"He that spares his rod hates his son: but he that loves him chastens him betimes"* (Proverbs 13:24).

> *"And, you fathers, provoke not your children to wrath: but bring them up in the nurture and admonition of the Lord"* (Ephesians 6:4).

In short, wise dads and moms establish their authority and love their kids. It can't be simpler than that. It takes a lot of brainpower and education to rear children using modern psychological techniques. I believe God has made it simple, and he has done so because he knows it is wisdom, not humanism, that is crucial to rearing children properly. God's wisdom is available to both the sophisticated and the simple if they are willing to search for it in His Handbook—The Bible.

The Slower Minded

Jake had suffered brain damage at birth that affected his ability to achieve academically beyond the sixth grade. Yet I have marveled at the practical wisdom he demonstrated when it came to interpersonal relationships. For Jake, if the Bible said something, that was the final authority—no discussion needed. Jake was also blessed with an exceptionally level head when it came to practical matters such as safety, cross-cultural communication, and child training. His slower mind did not hinder his application of practical wisdom; in fact, Jake married well. He had the wisdom to choose a godly woman who is sharper in areas where Jake is slow. Does she respect his God-given authority? Yes, she does.

Wisdom is superior to what is often called higher education. There are many educated fools. I have also come to the conclusion that quickness of mind is not necessarily indicative of mental superiority. The human mind is indeed complex, and it houses both the soul and spirit. I think we should keep this in mind when evaluating someone with a lower score on his IQ test.

Facing the Facts

I accept what the Bible says about the nature of children. They, by nature, are all of the following:

- Sinners. *"Behold, I was shapen in iniquity; and in sin did my mother conceive me"* (Psalm 51:5)
- Liars. *"The wicked are estranged from the womb: they go astray as soon as they be born, speaking lies"* (Psalm 58:3)

- Foolish. *"Foolishness (or rebellion) is bound in the heart of a child; but the rod of correction shall drive it far from him"* (Proverbs 22:15)

Since we know Solomon's words are true, then we understand why we must lovingly punish our children for rebellion, lying, disobedience, cheating, stealing, etc. He/she must pay a price for each offense immediately. No second warnings, and no delays. *"Because sentence against an evil work is not executed speedily, therefore the heart of the sons of men is fully set in them to do evil"* (Ecclesiastes 8:11).

"No warnings and no second chances?" You ask, incredulously. Yes, that's right. If you teach your child that he does not have to obey you the first time, you may find he doesn't obey you when he steps off a curb into the path of a car.

My faithful dad taught me to obey the first time. Not only was I spared tragedies, but I learned to obey others in authority, including my mother. Dad set the standards, and I praise God he did.

My dear mother though, had greater difficulties rearing two very active and creative boys—Ken and me. Perhaps it was because she was on call 24 hours a day that she would grow weary in well doing. Nevertheless, few mothers did a better job than our mom.

Mom had a weakness that was most evident when she would call us home from play. There were a series of signals that indicated how much time we had before we had to stop playing and head for home…fast!

"Biill-eeee!" She'd sing. "Dinner's on, and get'n cold!"

"Come'n," I'd yell. I knew I had at least 15 minutes more.

"Will-yum! I called you to dinner!"

"O.K. Mom, just a second!" I now had 10 minutes.

"William-Edward, you get in here! Dinner's on the table!"

"Come'n!" Now pressure was building. I had only 5 left.

"William-Edward-Pittenger, you'd better get in here this minute or I'm coming out there with a switch!!! Do you hear me?"

"I'm come'n, Mom!" Now I bee-lined for home knowing I'd face a very agitated mother.

Mom's approach contrasted dramatically with Dad's.

Dad would whistle. I would drop everything immediately and head for home. There was no second whistle, and no grace if I hesitated. Dad was always calm when I arrived. By the way, if Dad were home when Mom called, she needed call but once! There was something about Dad's authority and the way he administered it that demanded quick, submissive obedience.

Dad was a great teacher. When it came to teaching us to fish, hunt, shoot a gun, or work, he was superb! He was understanding and patient. Dad did not tolerate bad attitudes, and we respected him.

Take 'em on Early

My son Ricky was only two years old when he decided to take me on in a dining hall filled with Christians of all ages. I had dished out some vegetables on his high chair tray for him to eat. With mild defiance he responded, "Ugh!"

I said, "Ricky, eat your food."

He said more emphatically, "Uuuh!!"

I picked him up out of the high chair, took him out of the dining hall while everyone watched, and walked a discrete distance from the entrance. There I applied appropriate biblical methodology to the seat of Ricky's problem along with gentle words of love and admonition. We returned to the dining hall. Ricky was sniffling and wiping away a lingering tear.

I said, "Ricky, eat those vegetables." He remained defiant, arched his back, and articulated the same "Uuuh!"

We went out a second time, then a third time. Finally, after the fourth trip out, he submitted to my authority.

I am convinced that event was a turning point in Ricky's young life. He was never again defiant as far as I can remember. He was punished for other sins but not for willful disobedience. Today Rick is a firm believer in what I am teaching here. He and Kara are following God's Word in the training of their own children.

A child will repent if he receives the consequences for his behavior while he is young and tender. *"Train up a child in the way he should go: and when he is old, he will not depart from it"* (Proverbs 22:6).

If he repents and demonstrates a contrite heart, you have spared his soul from serious emotional pain when he passes through puberty and enters his teens. *"You shall beat him with the rod, and shall deliver his soul from hell"* (Proverbs 23:14).

If you wait until your son (or your daughter) is a teenager, it will be too late. He will have too many sinful habits already established and carry the burden of those habits throughout his life. It is common knowledge that the most critical formative years of a child are between birth and twelve years of age.

Shirley and I have observed many missionary families, and the majority of these homes have been exemplary. We noticed with interest the various philosophies of child training practiced by these missionaries and how their philosophies affected the lives of their children.

A few missionaries were permissive. They usually had self-willed, demanding, and rebellious children. Some missionary parents were, in my opinion, overbearing, but their apparent severity did not seem to result in serious problems in their children's behavior. The moms and dads who had a legalistic spirit though, had serious problems with their children, especially when those offspring were no longer living at home. Parents who were inconsistent in their training and families in which the mother assumed the headship also had problems with their children. The majority of missionaries followed the Scriptures' instructions. We rarely saw major problems in the lives of their children.

Spanking

The Bible says that if you love your child you will spank him. If you don't spank him it proves that you hate him. *"He that spareth his rod hateth his son: but he that loveth him chastenth him betimes"* (Proverbs 13:24).

I use this word "spank" because most of us know it means to inflict stinging pain to the buttocks using an appropriate instrument. Such an instrument would not bruise but rather cause a smarting sensation, a sting. The buttocks is the most appropriate and safest location to impose a pain that cures the soul. Proper spanking should not be labeled "child abuse." Extremists have sought to destroy the biblical model for training a child by excessive use of the word "abuse." Sadly, these people have gained the legal influence to enforce their radical philosophy. Therefore, spanking must be prudently administered in the privacy of your home, and you must plan ahead of time how you will control your child before entering a public place. You will be surprised at the variety of alternatives available to you.

Sensible people do not approve of battering or torturing a child. That behavior results in destruction of the child's respect and love for authority. It also results in injured children. Christians must never be guilty of such an act!

Why, then, does Solomon in Proverbs 13:24 use such strong words as "love" and "hate" in regards to the disciplining of your children? When dealing with the sins of your children, it might help you to remember the adage "No pain, no gain." *"Foolishness* (villainy) *is bound in the heart of a child; but the rod of correction shall drive it far from him"* (Proverbs 22:15). Consider what will happen if a child were left to do his own will. *"The rod and reproof give wisdom: but a child left to himself bringeth his mother to shame"* (Proverbs 29:15). Obviously, an undisciplined child will most certainly bring disgrace to his parents and himself (Cp. Proverbs 10:5; 19:26; 29:15). A father who permits his child to resist his authority is demonstrating to the world that he is more concerned about himself than he is about his child. Several motives may be behind this permissiveness—social pressure, philosophy, laziness, contempt, and feelings of inadequacy, to name a few. In all honesty, however, it boils down to neglect and a lack of love for his child. The word "spoiled" effectively describes what happens to a child who is not trained according to the biblical pattern. We have all observed children who show contempt for their dads, and who have disgraced their mothers.

Finally, and most importantly, a child who has the privilege of loving, consistent, and biblical discipline will *most likely* enjoy the following:

- Feel secure and loved
- Love both parents
- Respect authority—parental and civil
- Revere God and receive Christ as his Savior
- Become the Lord's disciple
- Experience success in whatever career he chooses

Conclusion

The "wisdom" of this modern age ruins children. Dr. Benjamin McLane Spock, the famous pediatrician of the 1940's and 50's, was thought to be wiser than Solomon. He had a reputation for providing common sense and hope for frustrated mothers by advising these insecure mothers to trust themselves to do the right thing—to follow their instincts. He opposed what was considered the authoritarian approach.

This authoritarian approach comprised the training methods commonly practiced in Christian homes before the 1950s. By encouraging mothers to do what seemed right to them at the time (Proverbs 14:12), Dr. Spock undermined the primary authority in the home. By focusing on mothers, he made a serious mistake, because the secret to rearing children properly rests with the father, not the mother. The father sets the standard in the home, and the mother carries out the father's objectives (Cf. Joshua 24:15 and Proverbs 1:8). Joshua set the standard for his home, and Solomon admonished a young man to accept the discipline (instruction) of his father and the commands of his mother.

We dads are the primary authority in our homes and we will not fail our sons or daughters if we fear offending God. We will not offend God if we follow His wisdom instead of popular theories. His wisdom will lead us to understand our wives and take advantage of their insights, and when we seek after wisdom as a miner seeks for gold, we will be rewarded. Fathers will save their children if we give ourselves to studying and applying the verses on child training. It is our responsibility to protect our homes from humanistic philosophies.

Many of my contemporaries were "Spocked" instead of trained. They, their kids and grandkids have reaped the consequences. In general, America is paying the consequences for following this false shepherd.

Chapter 20

MOTHERS
AND
THEIR CHILDREN

Her children arise up, and call her blessed;
her husband also,
and he praiseth her
Proverbs 31:28

I am fortunate to have a Proverbs 31 kind of wife. Shirley's children call her blessed, and I have many reasons to praise her. She is aware of her domestic power which she uses to strengthen the operation of the Pitt Ship.

Most of my colleagues in missionary service had wives like mine. I know of many others from all kinds of backgrounds who are Proverbs 31 types. These women are priceless! They understood their husband's needs and were willing to serve him and train their children. They knew the inestimable value of a full-time wife and mother. As the children grew to maturity, these mothers broadened their horizons and ministered to younger women or served in other ways—secretaries, teachers, nurses, counselors, musicians, etc. Many have found ways to increase the family income without compromising their domestic responsibilities.

One of these ladies was Shirley's mother, Helen Ayres Goddard. She married Bob Goddard, a restless man, who settled down only when they and their seven children arrived on a mission base in the heart of the Paraguayan Chaco—the so-called Green Hell I referred to earlier. Mom's life was anything but easy. She lived through The Great Depression and extreme poverty. She was a soldier's wife during World War II and after the war she followed Dad to New Tribes Mission's "bootcamp" where they lived in a tarpapered shack with their seven children. She suffered several miscarriages, at least one at bootcamp.

Mom has crossed the United States and traveled internationally many times. She knew isolation and learned two foreign languages. She washed clothes with a hand operated James Washer, cooked on a wood stove in 100 degree weather, and lived in an Indian style shack with split palm sides and dirt floors. Naked tribal people invaded her privacy even while she endured "the change of life." She saw her husband's life threatened by these people, but she still attended to their medical needs and sympathized with their sufferings. She did all that and more.

Why did she do it? She was loyal to her Savior and to her man, and she was Dad's best friend. She never spoke against him as far as we know.

Now, in her eighties, she is writing her autobiography of how God has blessed her life.

Dad has written four books—all with Mom's help. His best is his autobiography titled *Missionary Maverick* where he wrote how Mom knew how to use her domestic power to support Dad's objectives. They were indeed a team. Together they have taught God's Word to hundreds of people of several different Guaraní tribes. They have taught their fellow missionaries to speak Spanish and Guaraní—Paraguay's two national languages. Shirley's dad is a blessed man to have a wife like Helen Ayres Goddard—a powerful woman, indeed, even though she is five foot two and weighs about 98 pounds.

Influence is Power

I wanted to test my theory regarding a mother's superior domestic power in the home. So, I asked a teenaged girl this question, "Jennifer, who do the kids usually feel sorry for when there's a disagreement in your home, your mom or your dad?"

"Mom," she instantly replied.

From personal experience, I knew that would be her response. I suppose there are exceptions, but usually the children sympathize with their mother.

The Courts—Formal and Informal

It seems women have the upper hand in today's judicial courts. Consider who is most likely to receive custody of the children and alimony in today's divorce settlements. It takes a clever man to convince the world that he is a victim of a mother. If Dad were a victim of *any* woman, I doubt if very many people would feel sorry for him. Woe to the man that does not apprehend the domestic power of his "weaker vessel"—especially in Western cultures.

While shopping in Santa Cruz, Bolivia in 1987, I witnessed a public conflict between a heavyset peasant woman and a small wiry man. The man was only attempting to defend himself from her blows and fierce tongue-lashing.]** They were Quechua Indians, so I couldn't understand what was being said. It wasn't necessary. The skirmish was great entertainment for everyone watching, except me; I felt sorry for the man. He did not dare strike the woman in public because he would have gone to jail—Bolivia does not have a Taliban culture.

However, I knew things would have been different if there had been no witnesses. If the woman had been his wife, and had they been at home, she may have suffered a severe beating. Another Quechua man had told me beating a wife with a horsewhip was common. "How can a man control his wife if he doesn't beat her once in a while?" he told me. This philosophy may explain why that man's wife divorced him and married a gentler man.

Men have good reason to appreciate the power women have in the home and in modern society, but men are not powerless. By treating women and girls with proper respect we may enjoy their approval. The women in our lives can offer many blessings for those of us who treasure them.

Affirmative Power

To demonstrate how influential your wife is, imagine what happens when she says, "Honey, I am so glad I married you. I think you are the greatest. When I think of the other men I could have married, I cringe."

How would you feel if she said the following to your children? "You are fortunate that God gave you such a good dad. You should never speak against Dad to anyone because he is the head of this home." Her endorsement would do wonders in helping you be the father you hope to be.

The fact that our wives can affect us profoundly with positive affirmations demonstrates their influential role in the home. You may ask, "But isn't it also powerful when a husband and father affirms his wife?" Of course! But what happens if she does not affirm *you* before your children and other people? Worse, yet— what if she speaks negatively about you before your children and others?

One of the most significant illustrations of the power of affirmation was seen when Hilary Rodham Clinton, the former First Lady of our nation "stood by her man" publicly in spite the President's sexual indiscretions. Her support may have helped save his presidency.

First Lady Laura Bush, President George W. Bush's wife, is not often featured in the news, but when she is, it seems that President Bush's ratings in the polls go up. Gracious women don't have to say much to support their husbands. When they speak favorably about their husbands, the people are impressed.

From experience, I know many important executive matters are discussed in the bedroom. That's when a man's best friend, his wife, can advise and encourage her man to accept difficult challenges. Imagine how encouraging the following statement from your wife would be, "Dear, that project seems like a very big one to me. But, I know God has given you the wisdom and strength to do it. I'm with you, and if something goes wrong, just remember we're in this together!" If she has reservations, it might behoove you to carefully review your options.

We are blessed men indeed to have wives that are supportive of our objectives; interested in what we do for a living; delight in our friends; enjoy recreational activities with us; seek to share our dreams; and publicly commends us before others. We become more energized when they encourage us in our desire to take calculated risks.

A woman who knows the secret of encouragement is a wise woman indeed. I hope you have such a wife. You and your children will "rise up and call her blessed."

Spiritual Weapons

What if your wife—the mother of your children—is unwise? You may be in for some serious spiritual warfare. There's not much you can do to prevent it. However, you do have some powerful spiritual weapons and defenses at your disposal, but they are not the kind of weapons the world would use.

> *"For though we walk in the flesh, we do not war after the flesh: (For the weapons of our warfare are not carnal, but mighty through God to the pulling down of strong holds;) Casting down imaginations, and every high thing that exalteth itself against the knowledge of God, and bringing into captivity every thought to the obedience of Christ"* (II Corinthians 10:3-5).

Let's understand this passage: As Christ's disciple, you do not have the freedom to react with wrath, use insults, sneers, threats, etc. That is how one fights "in the flesh." How does one use God's weapons and pull down strongholds? The *truth* is in itself a powerful weapon. Calmly and gently use the truth to counter misconceptions and false assumptions. Carefully establish your position using truth and logic. Follow Christ's example. Be charitably kind, honest, and avoid guile even if your wife might be hateful and vicious *"[Christ] did no sin, neither was guile found in his mouth. [When] he was reviled, reviled not again; when he suffered, he threatened not; but committed himself to him that judgeth righteously"* (I Peter 2:22-23).

Gently counter the false statements and assumptions she makes. She may not accept correction; nevertheless, you have the authority to speak the truth graciously. If she rejects the truth, advise her that she is not resisting you, but Christ.

On the other hand, a wife does not have the authority to do this with her rebellious husband unless he asks her to speak. (See I Peter 3:1-6).

I Peter 2:23 actually tells us when Christ was persecuted He committed Himself to His Father for righteous justice. You might have to suffer at the hands of your wife just like Christ suffered at the hands of His Jewish countrymen and his own brothers (John 7:1-5). That included James who wrote a book in the Bible.

If you are persecuted for righteousness sake, you would have good reason to rejoice and be exceedingly glad. *"Blessed are ye, when men [and women] shall revile you, and persecute you, and shall say all manner of evil against you falsely, for my sake. Rejoice, and be exceeding glad: for great is your reward in heaven: for so persecuted they the prophets which were before you"* (Matthew 5:11-12).

If your attempts have failed, you can follow Christ's example and leave the matter in God's hands. Pray to your Heavenly Father. As the head priest of your home, intercede for your wife. You will have Christ interceding on your behalf as you do this (Hebrews 7:25-28).

You have the authority to rebuke your wife if you have your sins confessed. However, your rebuke could backfire.

The World vs. Women

Kosmos is the Greek New Testament word meaning "world order," and the word "world" is used in such verses as *"Love not the world..."* The world is one of our primary spiritual enemies. Our two other primary enemies are the flesh and the devil (Consider I John 2:15-17).

The world encourages women today to have careers of their own, live independently, and seek the same liberties enjoyed by men, including things that are simply not appropriate. The world says, "Stand up for your rights! You must defend yourself against a selfish husband. Get a good lawyer! Be your own person. Don't let anyone push you around." My response to those who follow such advice is, "Stay single and don't have children."

President Lyndon Johnson's "War on Poverty," the legislators' "no fault divorce," and the court's "Roe vs. Wade" has produced unprecedented increases of independent single women with children and the destruction of millions of pre-born children. Perhaps Johnson and our lawmakers thought they were doing good for our nation. Their policies, however, have undermined the family, and mass-produced single-parent and fatherless homes that depend on some form of government assistance. These results have been disastrous both for the children who died in abortion clinics and for those who were allowed to live. Satan is a vicious enemy, and he preys on people who forsake God's blueprint for living, especially Christians, who are his primary target. It is no wonder Paul wrote, *"And be not conformed to this world: but be ye transformed by the renewing of your mind, that ye may prove what is that good, and acceptable, and perfect, will of God"* (Romans 12:2). What you believe will affect what you do and your responses to your spouse.

If girls follow the feminist philosophy they will become foolish women. The Bible tells us that our world system (*kosmos**) has always been motivated by the devil to deceive us—both men and women. Today Satan, that old snake, is again telling the Eves of this world that God is holding out on them. Satan would have girls adopt Frank Sinatra's theme song "I Did It My Way." "Doing your own thing" is *iniquity* according to the Scriptures. *"As a jewel of gold in a swine's snout, so is a fair woman which is without discretion"* (Proverbs 11:22).

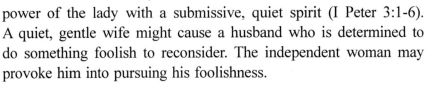

In contrast to the independent and self-willed woman, consider the power of the lady with a submissive, quiet spirit (I Peter 3:1-6). A quiet, gentle wife might cause a husband who is determined to do something foolish to reconsider. The independent woman may provoke him into pursuing his foolishness.

Mothers and Great Men

Someone said, "The hand that rocks the cradle rules the world." That statement may not be biblical, but the truth of that generalization cannot be ignored.

Several kings of Judah had evil fathers but godly mothers (See I and II Kings). You will notice that God often records the names of mothers of Judah's kings because they obviously played a major role in the development of the character of the child who would one day take the throne of King David. Similarly, Moses' mother trained Moses to be a Hebrew dedicated to God's people. She did this in spite of Moses' formal training in the highest levels of Egyptian culture. When the test came, Moses was a Hebrew, not an Egyptian. King Hezekiah had a horrible father in King Ahaz. Hezekiah became an exemplary king probably because of the faithfulness of his mother, Abi, the daughter of Zachariah the priest.

By contrast, there are examples of evil Israelite mothers, like Jezebel, who encouraged their sons to become evil and idolatrous leaders.

The Bible tells of many women who influenced the decisions of men of great authority. The story of Esther's influence over

King Ahasuereus is one of the most notable. Jews down through the centuries have celebrated a holiday called "Purim" because of their deliverance from annihilation. That miraculous deliverance, by God's grace, was brought about by the courage of this woman. Esther was a humble servant-wife to one of the world's most infamous heathen kings.

A prudent wife is indeed a powerful woman. *"House and riches are the inheritance of fathers: and a prudent wife is from the LORD"* (Proverbs 19:14). Give me that prudent wife and keep the house and riches!

In spite of the foolishness of the father of her children, a wise woman has the resources available to train her children to fear and follow the Lord. You will remember Timothy. Paul referred to his mother, Eunice, and grandmother, Lois, both Jewish women who trained Timothy to fear the Lord and understand the Scriptures (II Timothy 1:5). Timothy's father was a Greek. God honored these two women by including their names in our Holy Scriptures, but interestingly the name of Timothy's father is not there.

Dad's Weakness

It is a fact; most men are not brimming with godly wisdom. Spiritually, you may very likely be a common man. In fact, you could even be an unbeliever married to a Christian wife.

One of our former Christian students married a man who was an unbeliever. To complicate her life further, John had been married before. Because Amy was young and self-willed at the time, she married John even though the Bible clearly warns Christians not to be *"unequally yoked together with unbelievers"* (II Corinthians 6:14). John was a compliant man, and he allowed Amy to become the dominant figure in the home. Perhaps he had no alternative but to let her run things.

When the children came along she became even more domineering, and this resulted in her husband withdrawing further from any serious domestic leadership.

Amy attempted to train her children according to the Bible. With the help of her widowed Christian mother who came to live next door, she did a pretty fair job—except in regards to teaching her children to respect their father.

When the children were nearing their teens, they clearly had nothing but contempt for their father. At the same time, they dearly loved their mother and grandmother. Amy and her mother knew the children would suffer the consequences in some way or other if the children's contempt for the dad persisted.

Amy, Shirley, and I attended a seminar on personal relationships, and afterwards, we discussed what we were learning. Amy was anxious to know if she were doing things God's way. She asked us how she might win John to Christ. Amy obviously loved John. She was quick to point out that her husband was resourceful, a good provider, a hard worker, and generous toward her mother. However, she also had contempt for him because of his passivity, drinking habits, and general worldly lifestyle.

Amy was very concerned about the influence TV was having on her children. She told us emphatically, "I finally had to put my foot down regarding TV. I told the kids that from now on there would be no more TV during suppertime. That would be 'family time.' Then I turned to John and said, 'And that goes for you too, John!'"

Then Amy asked us, "What do you think of that?" Neither Shirley nor I felt good about it!

I asked Amy, "Does John call you 'the Old Lady" to his friends behind your back?"

She said, "I wouldn't be surprised, but he'd better not call me that around here!"

I asked, "Does he enjoy going to bars? And do you think he does that because of the tension at home?"

Amy said, "I wouldn't be surprised at that either!"

"Do the children respect their dad?"

"No way! They have no respect for him at all! In fact they pretty much ignore him."

Amy continued, "One day he was reading the riot act to Ronny, our son, and I told him, 'Don't you ever talk to my son that way again!' And believe me, he hasn't!"

I asked, "Did you know what John was so upset about?"

"Oh, kids stuff. The boys were fussing about something out in the pasture. You know, just fooling around like kids will do."

I asked Amy if she knew what young feisty boys might do that little girls would not think of doing. She wondered what I meant. Having been a boy, I told her what I had done without going into elaborate details, and I told her what my friends did who had temperaments similar to Ronny's. Shirley grew up with three brothers and other missionaries' boys, so she had a report of her own. Our stories made sense to Amy because she had brothers too. She only needed to be reminded.

Amy soon indicated a man's point of view might be helpful. She acknowledged her husband seemed to have a fair understanding of normal boys' behavior. She said, "John certainly knows how to deal with men in his business. He sure is accepted by his motorcycle gang." Nevertheless, she still objected to the way John had rebuked Ronny.

Eventually, Shirley and I were able to help Amy see how she had undermined John's authority in the home. She had judged his passive manner as simply being irresponsible. We suggested he might have chosen the only course available to him short of a divorce. Amy became very serious as she listened to us explain our understanding of these matters; what God's Word had to say about them; and how we worked them out in our own marriage. She asked, "What should I do?"

We encouraged Amy to ask for a family meeting. Once the family was gathered, including John, she could tell the family she had been taking John's authority away from him by calling the shots at home. She would then ask John's forgiveness by stating exactly what she had done to violate God's Word. Then, she was to turn to the children and explain what she was doing. She would, to best of her ability, try to let John take his position as the head of the home.

Amy said she would do just what we suggested. It would be hard, but she was prepared. She admitted that what she had been doing was ruining their home and marriage, even though John was perhaps guilty of more overt sins.

Some time later, Amy called and told us what had happened. When she had finished asking John to forgive her for usurping his authority, she turned to the children, Ronny and his sister Cynthia, and asked their forgiveness, too. She then made a promise, that to the best of her ability, she would be supportive of John's leadership. She covered many of the points we had discussed.

When she was through speaking, the children did something that surprised her. They ran to their dad and jumped up into his lap. They hugged and kissed him, and told him how much they loved him! Amy said she had never seen them express their love for him like that before!

Peace began to reign in that household. It continued until Amy went to a Bible study without consulting her husband—something she had promised she would not do. Later, in the privacy of their bedroom, John said, "Amy, you really didn't mean what you said, did you?"

Amy was shocked, "Of course I meant it. Why are you asking such a question?"

John reminded Amy of her agreement to involve him in deciding what Christian meetings she would attend. He wasn't doing this to control her. He said, "I thought you'd check with me when you wanted to go out. That way we could plan times to do things together." John thought Amy's reformation was too good to be true, and she had returned to being independent of him.

Amy asked John to forgive her again, and she reaffirmed her commitment to honor his position as head of the home.

The Quiet Ladies

Of course mothers vary in temperament, and you probably could easily discern that Amy was what some would call a "Type A" personality—vivacious, articulate, competent, and confident. No matter what your wife's temperament is, her influence on your family is great.

Quiet ladies also have very effective ways of influencing those near to them. One of my high school students had the most composed temperaments in the school of over 50 students. Jennifer had the highest grade point average in the history of the school, and she became valedictorian at her graduation. When the time came, her graduation speech was well thought out and delivered with remarkable composure.

As Jennifer sat in my history class of twenty-five students she rarely volunteered an opinion. She was alert, but serenely quiet. Her "Mona Lisa" smile and quiet dignity affected my behavior in that class!

I have a natural tendency to entertain my students. I used entertainment to help the students find history more appealing than the mind-numbing classes I had endured in high school and college. The danger is that an entertaining teacher must be alert to his audience, otherwise he could easily damage his effectiveness. Who do you suppose I looked to as the reflection of my effectiveness? Yes, you guessed it—Jennifer.

My concern about her response bothered me, but I had to accept this natural tendency. Jennifer rarely did more than produce her little smile, but that was all I needed to give me a sense of being on track. If that smile was not forthcoming, I immediately went into the self-examination mode and did a quick mental review of my past three or four statements. You might say Jennifer possessed "the power of the Mona Lisa smile." My wife, Shirley, has this same quality in her personality. When I am giving a public presentation I often will look at Shirley, hoping to find a Mona Lisa confirmation.

Criminal Husbands

Perhaps you agree that a mother is indeed a powerful influence in the home. You and I both realize that a foolish dad can destroy his marriage and his home, especially if he becomes unfaithful, or resorts to drunkenness, violence, gambling, or neglect. Frankly, in a marriage with such a person, a loyal wife and mother will have a very difficult, if not impossible, situation. Solomon has given us a very strong proverb that describes such a man: *He that troubleth his own house shall inherit the wind: and the fool shall be servant to the wise of heart* (Proverbs 11:29). Here is a paraphrase of this verse: *"A fool that stirs up trouble in his home will lose everything of lasting value, and end up serving a wiser person."*

I suspect many men who are considered "homeless" are among those who never learned the wisdom that would prevent provoking his family to wrath. It is so easy for a man to react and do something rash when he lacks wisdom, understanding, and self-control.

I want to make it clear here. I do not believe a wife and mother must tolerate criminal behavior. If a husband becomes an adulterer or engages in vices that destroy the home, I would urge the wife and mother to appeal to her own father for protection. If her father is unable to provide that protection, then she should go to her local church for help. Furthermore, criminal behavior must be reported to the police. God has given us these authorities to protect *true* victims. Certainly, a wife, mother, son, or daughter should appeal to our Heavenly Father, but remember He has established all authority, including civil authorities, for our protection (Romans 13:1, ff.).

Most Moms Mature

I am convinced your wife, the mother of your children, desires as much as you do to see your children trained according to biblical standards. Most Christian wives want their husbands to lead their homes spiritually. They want to support their husband's objectives and become more effective as wives and mothers. Like most of us, mothers are constantly growing in wisdom, knowledge and understanding. If they are young mothers, it will take time to learn how to apply the truths found in this book. Spiritual maturity is not accomplished by supernatural intervention, because God is in the character building business. Godly character and spiritual consistency are the result of the day-by-day application of God's Word.

Your wife will grow more quickly in wisdom, knowledge, and understanding if you are also applying truth to your own life. As she sees you mature in your service to your family, she will be motivated to apply God's truth to her own life.

With you and your wife functioning in your biblical roles, you have a good chance for success in preparing your sons and daughters for marriage to godly spouses. Your children should be more inclined to follow your example, and I hope they will seek to find marriage partners who will share the same convictions and practices. Moreover, you may have the privilege of being mentors to your future sons-in-law and daughters-in-law.

NOTES

PART IV

Let's assume you agree with the principles for order in the home discussed in Part III. We can now move on to the opinion saturated "science" of raising children in today's society. Fortunately, God has given us divine instructions to follow because opinions are not enough for such a serious matter.

In this brief section we will focus on another spiritual battle field in which the world, flesh, and devil will oppose any attempt to follow God's instructions. Therefore, I'll feature one faithful "warrior" whose training of his children resulted in the reproduction of succeeding generations of faithful children. However, he did not do this without the indispensable support of his wife.

Hopefully, you, like he, will also have an opportunity to see *your children* raising godly *grandchildren* who will delight you and your wife. Is it possible that one day your wife, children, grandchildren, and friends will call you blessed? *Children's children are the crown of old men; and the glory of children are their fathers* (dads) (Proverbs 17:6).

The Bible, of course, is in direct opposition to the destructive philosophies of child training and education. However it also addresses the pressures we and our children face regarding styles, entertainment, and acceptance. Therefore, in this section I'll seek to expose these powerful enemies that go for the souls of our children and grandchildren.

Let's put on the full armor of God, be courageous and "quit like men" because the rewards for faithfulness are wonderful in this life and the life to come.

For though we walk in the flesh, we do not war after the flesh: (For the weapons of our warfare are not carnal, but mighty through God to the pulling down of strong holds;) Casting down imaginations, and every high thing that exalteth itself against the knowledge of God, and bringing into captivity every thought to the obedience of Christ (II Corinthians 10:3-5).

OUTLINE OR PART IV

Chapter 21
TRAINING YOUR CHILDREN FOR MARRIAGE
From the Old School
Principles in Child Training
Spousal Unity
Advice from a Missionary Maverick

Chapter 22
TRAINING CHILDREN TO BE RESPONSIBLE
Home Bible Study
Mom's the Teacher and Dad's the Principal
Young Adult Children
Sex Education
Young Adults and the World
The Enemy is Cultural and Political
There's a Great Day Coming
It's Not an Easy Road

CHAPTER 21

TRAINING YOUR CHILDREN FOR MARRIAGE

Train up a child in the way he should go:
and when he is old, he will not depart from it
Proverbs 22:6

If you have confidence in the wisdom of God regarding raising children, you have a good chance for success in helping your children marry well. However, since human beings have wills of their own, and because they are born with a sinful nature, no one can guarantee success.

If you believe that you are not qualified to go against our culture, I have good news for you. You can do it. In fact, you are called to do battle against the world. The Gospel, itself, is contrary to the wisdom of this world and is considered foolishness (See I Corinthians 1:23). The Holy Spirit is dwelling in you; you have God's Handbook for godly living; and you have the desire to obey His prompting (Romans chapters 6 and 8). Furthermore, you have godly people who can help you find Scriptures that cover every problem you will encounter.

> *And he gave some, apostles; and some, prophets; and some, evangelists; and some, pastors and teachers, for the perfecting of the saints, for the work of the ministry, for the edifying of the body of Christ: till we all come in the unity of the faith, and*

> *of the knowledge of the Son of God, unto a perfect*
> *man, unto the measure of the stature of the fulness*
> *of Christ* (Ephesians 4:11-13).

And God will give wisdom to anyone who asks.

> *If any of you lack wisdom, let him ask of God, that*
> *giveth to all men liberally, and upbraideth not; and*
> *it shall be given him. But let him ask in faith, nothing*
> *wavering. For he that wavereth is like a wave of the*
> *sea driven with the wind and tossed* (James 1:5-6).

I don't care how bad you've been, how ignorant you are of the Bible, or how fearful you are. You can begin overcoming these things, immediately. Just don't put it off. Ask God for wisdom and determination. He promised to give these to you. Most importantly, by all means, for your children and their children's sake, start training your kids the best you can. After all, you can't be worse off than the tribal people in the jungles of Bolivia. Many of those people are now Christians, and they are teaching their children using God's Word. If "primitive" peoples can follow the principles taught in God's Word, then any Christian can do so.

From the "Old School"

I believe the best thing I can do is to tell you in more detail what Shirley and I did to prepare our children for marriage. We know you will do things somewhat differently than we did. I hope you will follow the principles of Scripture as closely as you can.

First, we admit we have an advantage over many because our parents did a good job in training us from early childhood. They followed the Bible in regards to discipline and love. I cannot recall one time that I was disciplined unjustly; in fact, I received fewer spankings than I deserved. I was spanked on that meaty area

I sit on that is located just behind my lap. My "bee-hind" took the swats without any physical injury, though my pride suffered dearly because I did not lack self-esteem. My self-esteem and self-centeredness came at conception (Psalm 51:5).

Always, with the spanking, I received assurances of Mom and Dad's love. During the war years, while my brother and I were living with Grandma Pittenger and my Aunt Aletha Pittenger, that same form of loving, godly discipline and instruction continued until we were able to rejoin our parents.

Shirley was raised under the same form of "nurture and admonition of the Lord" as I, so she was an asset, not a hindrance, to the training of our children.

Both of our parents' homes were considered "patriarchal," which means Dad was the recognized authority in the home. Mom supported Dad in regards to child training; Dad made the final decisions when there was no clear agreement. The "buck" stopped with Dad. Some people would say we were from the "old school." We believe we are from "God's school," and that our parents were good instructors by word, example, and action. We were fortunate to receive such love.

Someone said to me, "Good for you! But our Christian counseling centers are filled with adults who, as children, were abused by parents or in missionary children's homes."

If you are picking up a justification for cruel punishment of children from what I have written, I have not expressed myself clearly enough. There certainly exist violations of God's standards in Christian homes and institutions. Books, articles, and TV specials have focused on "the seemingly pandemic" abuse of children and women. Does this reflect the consequences of following God's instructions or man's philosophies? My Bible teaches against injustice, violence, and cruelty. It is the philosophies of man that pressure societies away from God's wisdom.

It seems like people in the "new school" are not doing so well according to the daily news reports. You might say, "Many in the old school didn't do very well either." Of course you'd be right because parental failure goes back to Adam. However, I believe the records show that permissiveness has been more harmful to children than the loving discipline advocated by Solomon and the Apostle Paul.

Our parents were faithful in church attendance and Bible study, and they were active in serving their Savior in a variety of ways. Best of all, they lived what they believed. Shirley and I have endeavored to follow this Bible-centered tradition, and our children continue to do the same. Have we ever failed? You know the answer to that. Certainly! I've told you plenty about us already, so you know we are in the same boat as the rest of Adam's fallen family. That's why we need daily doses of God's wisdom (See Psalm 119:11).

My brother and I grew up going to church and learning the fear of God. This fear of God eventually led both of us to put all of our trust in Christ and His great salvation.

You may not have had these advantages, but you are willing to learn. The Bible is available to you, and with prayerful determination you can quickly learn the key principles of child training. I have friends who came from very poor backgrounds who have trained their children God's way. My own father came from a broken home, yet he trained my brother and me very effectively even though he never graduated from high school.

If you are one of those people who have less than a college education, or less formal education than your wife, I have good news for you. Institutional or "formal" education is not a reflection of your intelligence or your abilities as a man. Everyone receives an education; it is an ongoing process throughout your life. So-called "institutions of higher learning" may give you certain tools, but they must be applied to be profitable. However, apprenticeships, on the job training, self-education, research and personal discipline are wonderful ways to get a profitable education. The best education, however, must include the knowledge, understanding and application of God's Word.

Thou through thy commandments
hast made me wiser than mine enemies: for they are ever with me.
I have more understanding than all my teachers:
for thy testimonies are my meditation.
I understand more than the ancients,
because I keep thy precepts
(Psalm 119:98-100)

Principles in Child Training

Because you have read this book to this point, I'm convinced you will do well. You will nurture, encourage, rebuke, correct, chasten, admonish, and do whatever it takes to train your children biblically. You love your Lord, and you desire to be faithful in training *His* children He entrusted to you.

Therefore, you will:

- Teach your child to fear and reverence God (Proverbs 9:10)
- Teach your child that God established parental authority (Genesis 18:19)
- Establish your authority (Proverbs 29:15)
- Accept God's order of authority—Father, Son, Dad, Mom, children (Cp. I Corinthians 11:3)
- Begin training earlier than you expected (Proverbs 19:18).
- Not permit your child to manipulate you (Proverbs 19:18)
- Train your infant to understand "no" (Psalm 51:5-6)
- Train your toddler not to cry selfishly—whining (Hebrews 12:5-12)
- Insist that your child adjusts to your schedule—sleeping, eating, and attention (Hebrews 12:5-12)
- Win every battle because your child is young and foolish (Proverbs 22:15)
- Expect your child to obey immediately without a second chance (Proverbs 23:13-14)

- Make your child pay with pain for self-centered and selfish conduct (Proverbs 23:13)
- Not tolerate bad attitudes—neither yours nor your children's (Ephesians 6:4)
- Actively love your child even when you don't feel like it (Hebrews 12:6-8)
- Give assurances, hugs, and caresses following painful discipline (Colossians 3:21)
- Listen to your child at your convenience, not the child's convenience (Cp. Galatians 4:1-2)
- Resist popular philosophies on child training that contradict the Bible (Colossians 2:8)
- Expect your child to respect people and their property (Cp. Psalm 58:3 with Psalm 51:5)

You may find it difficult to put the principles into practice because of various pressures. Keep in mind, though, that many people who were not properly trained as children have succeeded in training their own children.

The stakes are high indeed. We are entrusted with the training of people who will live forever, and we have an enemy who understands this! A rock n' roll star said to a news reporter, "We are going for the souls of your children." Like the rock star, who represents "the world," Satan too is going after the souls of our children. Our enemies—the world, the flesh and the devil—may be strong, but we have our Creator on our side.

Spousal Unity

> *"And if one prevail against him, two shall withstand him;*
> *and a threefold cord is not quickly broken"*
> Ecclesiastes 4:12

The value of spousal unity in our parents' homes, as well as ours, cannot be underestimated. My dad, Shirley's dad, and I will admit that the indispensable factor to success in rearing godly children has been the willingness of our wives to follow our leadership. We were all far from being clever leaders, but as we followed Christ and His Word, so too did our wives follow Christ, His Word, and us, their husbands. If our wives had chosen to follow the trends of our American culture, our families might be in ruins today. (Could the third strand represent the children who follow their mother's example of submission to dad's authority? A family thus united is strong indeed).

Advice from a Missionary Maverick

In these pages I said our parents did a credible job of training us biblically. Shirley and I followed their example, and our children are following what we have handed down to them. Therefore, it seems fitting that you read "How to Raise Kids Biblicaly," by Shirley's rough-hewn dad, Robert C. Goddard. Here are portions of that article.

Being 82 years of age and of sound mind, I have been privileged in my lifetime to observe some of the results of letting a child express himself. Somewhere along the line, the American people have traded the Bible for psychology when it comes to child raising. Instead of "spare the rod and spoil the child," we now say, "spare the rod and let the child express himself"—and he does!

As a father of seven kids, I speak with at least some knowledge. When our baby was fed, changed and put back in his crib, he started to cry. He was saying if I didn't pick him up and put him in bed with us, he would cry all night. After a futile attempt at sleeping, I picked him up. The crying stopped with a couple of hiccups. After I had assured myself there was nothing physically wrong with him, I "spatted" him a couple of times, put him back in the crib where he put on a good show. I picked him up again and repeated the process. I think it was the third time he got the picture. I placed him gently in the crib. He stuck his thumb in his mouth and went to sleep.

I am glad I didn't have the help of "experts" in raising my kids. They say, "ignorance is bliss," and I was ignorant of modern psychology. I just didn't know any better. I guess I raised kids with "horse sense." Or as our pilots in Paraguay [said] before they had all of the fancy instruments they have nowadays, "We flew by the seat of our pants—by sight and dead reckoning." That's something like the way I raised my kids—by sight and dead reckoning. I did have a Bible, however, and found most of what I needed for running the family circus!

Of seven, five are missionaries and the other two are law abiding, respectable citizens, of the good old USA.

Until our kids left home they were taught by corporal punishment not to sass their parents, to do their chores, and act more or less civilized around the house. They grew up, for the most part, among the Indians of Paraguay, so they didn't have the bad influence of some of our civilized kids. The bad habits of the Indian kids didn't affect ours much— since they just considered the source.

We even had one who was "abnormal." I don't remember that I ever had to spank her! One time when she was about three years old, her older sister was blowing off some verbal steam. The younger one got worried and said to her sister, "Hush up! Daddy said, *'Be quiet or I'll spank you!'*" Yes, there are exceptions to all rules and some kids are different. That's where common sense enters the picture. You don't chastise a kid for a physical defect such as partial deafness, dyslexia, or any other such problems.

When we went to Paraguay, many good folks were convinced we would self-destruct. They thought our kids would grow up ignorant. Obviously, that didn't happen, and the kids got a better education than they would have received in the USA. They got in on history before it was re-written, and they lived geography. They all speak at least one foreign language. They observed the Indian and Paraguayan cultures first hand and learned the social graces of both. Probably the greatest blessings in raising our kids was the absence of television. Instead of television, they became avid readers.

Since most of you will not be able to emulate us in our career, the best I can do is advise you. Bring your kids up with the Bible as your guide. See that your kids obey you, and enforce your instructions without doing physical harm. My father used a razor strap. It didn't leave anything but a warm posterior, a sense of humility, and a respect for parental authority.

The experts say never chastise your child while you are angry. I heartily disagree. You can do a better job if you show the kid your displeasure, and it adds inspiration to do the job! If you spank him with a forced smile on your face he will think you are just playing. A word of caution: don't get so mad you lose your control. It's a good idea to count to ten before you act, but don't wait too long or you lose momentum, and the kid might forget what he's getting spanked for.

Well, I reckon that about winds up my advice on raising kids. It's the best this old maverick can do for you.

Signed, *Robert C. Goddard* 3/12/99.

It is refreshing to recall the days when raising children was not considered complicated. Those were the days when dads were expected to be the head of the homes in America and moms were expected to support their husband's leadership. Those were also the days when Christians believed the Bible was the final authority in *"all things that pertain to life and godliness"* (II Peter 1:3).

Chapter 22

TRAINING CHILDREN TO BE RESPONSIBLE

Now I say, That the heir, as long as he is a child,
differeth nothing from a servant, though he be lord of all;
But is under tutors and governors until
the time appointed of the father.
Galatians 4:1-2

Let us assume we are in consistent fellowship with our spouses, have established our parental authority, and we are following biblical principles in training our children of all ages. We are ready to prepare them for the last stages of their in-home-training—post puberty.

Home Bible Study

Every family will have a different way of teaching and applying the truth of God's Word. Some dads like a regular, scheduled, family time of Bible study with their wives and children. Others are less structured. The important thing is to "feed" your family spiritually, emotionally, intellectually, and physically in a loving manner. The attitude in which the father leads his family is what matters—an attitude that is in keeping with the Holy Spirit. *But the fruit of the Spirit is love, joy, peace, longsuffering, gentleness,*

goodness, faith, meekness, temperance: against such there is no law (Galatians 5:22-23).

All of my adult life I have been admonished to be a good listener, and each admonition was needed and heeded ... well, most of the time. I had to be reminded to listen to Shirley and to each of the children. As natural as it may be, it is foolish to disregard those you love the most, just as it is wrong to ignore, or "check out" on anyone else. Proverbs 18:13 says, *"He that answereth a matter before he heareth it, it is folly and shame unto him."*

Mom's the Teacher and Dad's the Principal

The home is the best place to teach children the following:

- How to work with their hands
- How to develop their talents so as to be skilled in a variety of areas
- How to develop self-discipline
- How to complete tasks
- How to remain focused on high priorities

There simply is no higher calling than the ministry of training your children. Properly trained children respect their parents when they are adults.

> *"The rod and reproof give wisdom: but a child left to himself bringeth his mother to shame"* (Proverbs 29:15).

Since this is true, a properly trained child will not disgrace his mother, while permissiveness will encourage a child to do so.

Mom will do more of the day-by-day and hour-by-hour training, but Dad has the oversight. Dad is the captain of the family ship, whether at home or at work. The executive officer (Mom) will have a list of reports for the captain (Dad) to evaluate each day. The captain will discuss these matters with his exec and, with her input, make decisions that will encourage smooth sailing. A wise captain never brushes off his executive officer's reports on the state of the ship and the ship's crew. In addition, the captain never second-guesses his executive officer in the presence of the crew. A smoothly run ship has a captain and executive officer who are respectfully loyal to one another.

By being loving authorities in training their children, Dad and Mom will see their children develop into responsible adults. The kids will study in school and know how to work physically; they will be respectful toward people, especially those in authority; and they will trust Dad and Mom in helping them choose a godly spouse.

Young Adult Children

Assuming your children—ages 13 and older—have been properly trained, we can move into this all-important subject of finding a godly spouse. If they have not been properly trained, you can only hope to instruct them. If they are receptive, you may succeed in spite of circumstances. Believe me; it is certainly worth a try to get them to follow the instructions in this book.

When our daughters entered young adulthood at the ages of 12, 13, or 14, they had been fairly well prepared for young adult challenges by a variety of people such as parents, teachers, peers, relatives, and others. They experienced the emotional roller coaster rides that came with puberty, but we were there to help. However, we also had to face the fact that there is only so much parents can do. We had to learn to leave much of their training to the Great Shepherd who loves His sheep much more than we do.

After puberty, physical discipline for rebellion and disobedience had come to an end for the most part, and by that time, our children were ready for adult-level instruction. Our son still needed some physical discipline during his early years of adulthood, but it was administered with his reluctant cooperation.

If your children have not learned to respond to correction by the time they are 14, you have a serious challenge on your hands.

However, prayer remains your principal resource. Of course there are varieties of ways your authority can be exercised, such as the withdrawal of privileges, "speaking the truth in love," rebuking, and warning.

Sex Education

The sex education of our children was our responsibility, not that of the church and *certainly not* of the school. We covered that delicate subject with our children prior to puberty, beginning incrementally very early in their lives. Because of their knowledge, they did not need the instruction of others outside the home, even though there were those who attempted. I'm sure our kids received much information on the subject from their peers, and possibly others; for parents to guard their children from all sources of undesirable influence would be impossible. Nevertheless, Shirley and I had taught them first. By the age of 12, each of our children was prepared for the changes that would take place in their bodies at puberty.

Children who have reached this age of reproduction are in the final stretch to marriage, and what a critical time that is! No wonder the enemy of our souls pulls out all of the stops to entice early teens into destructive relationships that would soil their character. Early adulthood is definitely not the time to ease up on our influence in our children's lives. They need Dad's oversight and Mom's affirmation more than ever. They need to see that Mom and Dad love one another and are loyal to each other.

Young Adults and the World

Our daughters experienced strong peer pressure regarding styles of dress as soon as they passed over the puberty line. Peers didn't affect Rick's choice of clothes quite as much, but he was aware of what was "cool."

Some mothers of our daughters' peers put subtle pressure on Shirley to dress our daughters to look cute, cool, sexy, and/ or fashionable. The "in group" seemed to oppose modest clothing styles. If we had not been alert, our daughters could have easily been influenced to dress in a way that draws attention to their bodies, not their personalities and character.

The following styles have been paraded before the entire population during the past few decades:

- Tight jeans and tank tops
- Bikinis
- Summer short-shorts
- Nipple imprints on tight halters
- Mini-skirts and pink panties
- Oversized clothing that goes with slumping, shuffling, and an attitude
- Bulging breasts above a tight top
- Low-cut tops to show cleavage
- The knotted blouse with exposed belly button
- Short top with exposed belly button
- Ruby red lips, or blackberry, grape, or gray lips, and much more
- Eyes encircled with black
- Unnaturally designed eyebrows
- Body piercing

Shirley and I taught our children *why* people would fall in line with these trends.

The Enemy is Cultural and Political

We have a very powerful enemy who desires to destroy us all, including our sons and daughters. Therefore, Shirley and I taught our children that their outward appearance gave testimony as to whom they served. Satan's world wants to paint, decorate, and dress them so that they would blend in with his system.

It's important to remind fathers, mothers, sons and daughters of all ages that our battles on earth are short, and that eternity is a long time. The stakes are high indeed!

There's a Great Day Coming

*"The day of the Lord will come as a thief in the night;
in the which the heavens shall pass away with a great
noise, and the elements shall melt with fervent heat,
the earth also and the works that are therein shall be
burned up. Seeing then that all these things shall be
dissolved, what manner of persons ought ye to be in
all holy conversation and godliness? Looking for and
hasting unto the coming of the day of God—the heavens
being on fire shall be dissolved, and the elements shall
melt with fervent heat. Nevertheless we, according to
his promise, look for new heavens and a new earth,
wherein dwelleth righteousness. Wherefore, beloved,
seeing that ye look for such things, be diligent that
ye may be found of him in peace, without spot, and
blameless"* (II Peter 3:10-14).

Knowing this, we tremble not at what our enemy will try to do to us but focus on that blessed day when our Lord Jesus Christ shall come for His Bride. We look to that Great Day when we, His saints, shall return with Him, to reign over the world from Jerusalem. His Second Coming will be with such a dramatic display that the people of the world will be terrified—but not us, because we shall be with Him!

*Wherefore, beloved, seeing that ye look for such things, be
diligent that ye may be found of him in peace, without spot, and
blameless*
II Peter 3: 14

It's Not an Easy Road

Raising children and preparing them for marriage is not an easy task, but it is the highest calling God has given fathers and mothers. I believe it is a higher calling than making disciples of people outside the immediate family. If we develop the art of making disciples of our own children, we will be better prepared to make disciples of others. When our children follow us as we follow our Lord, they, in turn, will train their children and others (Consider II Timothy 2:2).

> *And let us not be weary in well doing: for in due season we shall reap, if we faint not. As we have therefore opportunity, let us do good unto all men especially unto them who are of the household of faith* [including our children] (Galatians 6:9-10 and comment added).

The window of opportunity with our children is very small compared to the years that precede and follow their residence with us. Therefore, let us "redeem the time," for the rewards for faithfulness are eternal.

NOTES

NOTES

Printed in the United States
84489LV00006B/277-348/A